When Dogs Heal

JESSE FREIDIN / ZACH STAFFORD / CHRISTINA GAROFALO / DR. ROBERT GAROFALO

When Dogs Heal

POWERFUL STORIES OF PEOPLE LIVING WITH HIV AND THE DOGS THAT SAVED THEM

ZEST BOOKS
MINNEAPOLIS

Zest Books™
An imprint of Lerner Publishing Group, Inc.
241 First Avenue North
Minneapolis, MN 55401 USA

For reading levels and more information, look up this title at www.lernerbooks.com.
Visit us at zestbooks.net.

Design elements by: zo3listic/Shutterstock.com; miomilka/Shutterstock.com.

Designed by Kimberly Morales.
Main body text set in Century Schoolbook Std.
Typeface provided by Monotype Typography.

Library of Congress Cataloging-in-Publication Data

Names: Freidin, Jesse, 1981- photographer. | Garofalo, Robert (Pediatrician), author.
Title: When dogs heal : powerful stories of people living with HIV and the dogs that saved them / Jesse Freidin, Dr. Robert Garofalo, Zach Stafford, Christina Garofalo.
Description: Minneapolis : Zest Books, [2021] | Audience: Ages 13–18 | Audience: Grades 10–12 | Summary: "When Dogs Heal is a beautiful, unique collection of full-color portraits and personal accounts of love, connection, and survival, showcasing HIV-positive people who are thriving and celebrating life, thanks to the compassion and unconditional love of their dogs"— Provided by publisher.
Identifiers: LCCN 2019060014 (print) | LCCN 2019060015 (ebook) | ISBN 9781541586734 (library binding) | ISBN 9781541586765 (paperback) | ISBN 9781728414621 (ebook)
Subjects: LCSH: HIV-positive persons—Biography. | HIV-positive youth—Biography. | Dogs. | Human-animal relationships.
Classification: LCC RC606.54 .F74 2021 (print) | LCC RC606.54 (ebook) | DDC 362.19697/920092 [B]—dc23

LC record available at https://lccn.loc.gov/2019060014
LC ebook record available at https://lccn.loc.gov/2019060015

Manufactured in the United States of America
1-47426-48005-6/19/2020

This book is dedicated to the memory of Tremaine Bradley, one of the most beautiful, radiating people we had the pleasure of meeting while working on the *When Dogs Heal* photo exhibit. Without knowing who we were, Tremaine jumped on a subway one day in New York and rushed to the photography studio, simply because his heart was so open and he was willing to share his experience and joy with the world. He wanted his story to make a difference. Tremaine passed away at the age of twenty-six, soon after we met him.

CONTENTS

Introduction

BY JESSE FREIDIN, PHOTOGRAPHER

Jesse with Pancake

When I was growing up, I faced an incredible amount of adversity and rejection that darkened my whole world, because not only was I a left-handed, daydreaming blond kid with a bowl cut—I was visibly queer. I couldn't hide it, and I couldn't help it. Without role models to tell me that it was okay to be who I was, I became weighed down with stigma and negative thoughts.

As I got older, I learned that there were so many other interesting people in the world just like me. It simply took some digging to find them. I also learned that being different made me stronger. It gave me a perspective that helped me find my voice both creatively and personally. Now as an adult, I get the opportunity to help queer youth understand that just because they are not being loved by their family or community does not mean that they are unlovable. When I was young, I felt safest spending time with dogs. Dogs never judged me for how I looked or what I believed in. They simply let me get close to them and be myself. It didn't matter what I was wearing or how I identified—I was always a complete and worthy person in the eyes of a dog and that connection deeply affected me. For that reason, the message that dogs heal us is foundational to this project and to so much of my photographic work as a whole. Dogs ground us, dogs stick with us and dogs provide the strongest of cures—unconditional love.

The portraits in this book carry a deep message of acceptance, one that I hope readers will amplify. The future can be a place where hatred has no home, but only if young people continue to replace negative messages with their own beautiful stories of truth and positivity. If *When Dogs Heal* inspires just one of you to continue that work, the photographs will have succeeded.

There is great power in turning a stigmatizing narrative on its head. My aim in developing this series with Dr. Garofalo over a span of six years was to show people with HIV thriving, loving and being loved—a visual story that is rarely told. The fact that I, a queer artist, can take the narrative away from people who believe HIV is a terrifying and shameful plague, and illustrate an honest, positive and beautiful experience of this terrible disease means that we are in an era when young people are free to take control of their own stories. And that's a beautiful moment to be alive.

Those of you who are young adults today no longer need to live in a world where difference is dangerous and stigma keeps you silent. That world is over.

This is what I hope this book will inspire you to do:

Get out and fight for queer rights.

Spread a message of love and acceptance.

Create safe spaces for all kinds of marginalized people.

Take control of the conversation.

Erase stigma.

That is how we can change the world.

Oh, and get a dog!

Introduction

BY DR. ROBERT GAROFALO

As a pediatrician at Ann & Robert H. Lurie Children's Hospital of Chicago and professor of pediatrics at Northwestern's Feinberg School of Medicine, I have devoted my career to helping adolescents and young people cope with and manage being diagnosed and living with HIV. But in 2010, the unexpected happened. I tested HIV positive. I felt like a failure. I felt damaged, ashamed and alone. I didn't eat. I had trouble sleeping. I was a mess. I had always prided myself on being a silly, goofy, fun-loving guy, but following my HIV diagnosis every day was a struggle. I was somehow unable to afford myself the same compassion I had spent my career giving to others. I saw my life slipping away. I knew I needed to take back control—I just didn't know how.

In early 2011, I took an unorthodox first step toward healing. On a frigid winter day, I rented a car and drove to Gurnee, Illinois, and adopted a ten-week-old Yorkie puppy I named Fred. Choosing to adopt Fred was an impulsive decision. It was not even quite rational. I had never had a pet before. I knew nothing of caring for a dog. I could barely care for myself. What in that moment made me think a dog was the answer? But I knew I was in deep trouble. I knew I needed to do something. And looking into that puppy's eyes, I knew I had to have him.

It wasn't instantaneous, it took some time, but over the ensuing weeks and months, Fred brought me back to life. With boundless energy, a pure soul and unconditional love, he was the perfect antidote to the isolation and loneliness that crippled me. He had no patience for self-pity. He just wanted to be loved and, more importantly, to love me. Fred brought peace and joy back to my life, when I thought that neither were possible again. With Fred by my side, I felt unstoppable . . . ALIVE. To me, he was magic. And with healing came power. Suddenly I wanted to give back to my community and share that magic with others. I wanted to create something personal that tied together my personal journey and my life's work of helping to care for teenagers affected by and living with HIV.

So in 2012, I started Fred Says, a nonprofit charity I named after my dog, and began using Fred, social media, local events such as the Ride for AIDS Chicago and strategic partnerships with Stonewall Sports Chicago and other organizations to raise funds to improve the lives of young people living with HIV. I knew I had been given a gift in Fred, and I wanted to share that gift with the world. Fred had given me back my life, and together we were going to make the world a better place. To date, Fred Says has raised and given back more than $300,000 to community agencies in Chicago and across the United States that care for HIV-positive teens.

On a fall day the following year I traveled to Los Angeles with my friend and colleague Zach Stafford, as part of a charity event honoring Fred Says. While we were there, Zach and I decided to pay a visit to Jesse Freidin, an acclaimed pet photographer and friend I had met a few years earlier. The three of us talked about the challenges facing Fred Says, of how to leverage social media to fundraise, by connecting a dog (in this case, Fred) to the broader mission of a nonprofit charity supporting those affected by and living with HIV. We struggled for a bit until suddenly, I knew I had it. "When Dogs Heal!" I blurted out. It was in that moment this project was born. Unlikely partners—a pediatrician, a writer and a photographer—we sat there, thinking creatively and ultimately envisioning a project where we would travel the country and tell stories of real people living with HIV and their dogs, using both photography and narrative to capture the healing power these amazing animals have in helping those grappling with a stigmatized, often chronic, and sometimes deadly disease. Along the way we added my niece Christina Garofalo to our team to help with the interviews and writing. From the beginning, I knew we had a dream team to bring this to life.

Our first stop on this journey was Chicago. Then trips to San Francisco, New York, Los Angeles and Atlanta followed. Each of our lives were busy with other things, but we found the time and made it happen. We traveled on a shoestring budget, often staying with friends and using whatever connections we had to find spaces conducive to a photo shoot. We contacted agencies in each city that served HIV-positive young people and asked case managers and health-care providers to help us identify clients who may have shared powerful stories about their dogs during clinical encounters. Zach and I sat in coffee shops using apps such as Grindr and Scruff to reach out to HIV-positive people. Finding people was NOT easy. Nor was convincing them to do the project. We needed to find people who were HIV positive, willing to be open and talk about their HIV status with total strangers, had dogs and a compelling story to tell about how their dogs had helped them cope with and manage living with HIV, were willing to come to a photo shoot and were willing to make all of that public by way of an art exhibit and now this book. One of my good friends summed it up this way: "Good luck! That's like trying to find a unicorn." But find them we did. The people you will see and read about in these pages wanted their stories to be told. They trusted us with their stories. And we knew we had to tell them.

Whether it was Paulo and his dog Stud in Chicago, Lynnea and Coconut in Los Angeles, Brad and Thor in San Francisco, Michelle and her daughter Raven with their dog Couture in New York, RJ and Stoli in Atlanta or any of the other wonderful people who honored us by participating, each person and dog was unique. Yet common themes recurred. About hardships and overcoming them. About hurt and healing. About fear of dying, yet surviving and thriving. About LOVE. Combining Jesse's sweet and pure images with stories that were raw and emotional proved powerful. Sometimes the stories are hard to read because of the emotions they invoke, but the stories—the lives—these participants shared with us are at their core uplifting and full of heart. They are stories that Jesse, Zach, Christina and I hope will inspire readers and make a difference to young people living with HIV.

A Gift All the Same

JOSEPH & PANCAKES

One rainy October night, I got off the bus near my home in Chicago to find a cute, curly-haired puppy staring up at me. She wasn't on a leash but wore a collar and was well-groomed. I assumed her owner was nearby, but no one was in sight. As I started walking toward my apartment, she followed me all the way to my front porch.

A group of friends were waiting there for a gathering I'd planned, but I didn't want to leave the dog outside in the bad weather. I went down the block to ask a few of my neighbors if they recognized her or knew the owners, but no one had seen her before. I decided to bring her inside just until the rain stopped, and then I would try to locate her owner.

She seemed nervous when I brought her in; she didn't leave my side the entire evening and wouldn't eat anything I offered her. At the end of the night, after everyone left, I climbed into bed and she immediately jumped in after me and cuddled up close. The next morning, we woke to my roommate making pancakes. I could sense she was hungry, so I offered her a piece and that was the first thing she ate. That's how Pancakes got her name.

My friends joked, "I guess you've got yourself a dog now," but I was adamant that I'd find where she belonged. I loved dogs but felt like I wasn't in a place where I could take on that responsibility. My apartment didn't even allow dogs! For the next month, I worked to locate her owners. I filed a report with 311 and local groomers to see if anyone reported a missing dog; no one had. I brought her to the vet to see if she was microchipped; she wasn't. The only responses to my posts on social media and signs in the neighborhood were from creepy people who definitely didn't know her. After a month with no viable leads, my roommate and I figured she should stay with us. Despite my initial hesitation, Pancakes turned out to be exactly what I needed.

Two months earlier, I had been diagnosed with HIV. My partner of two years wanted to have an open relationship, and even though I wasn't on board, I felt beholden to what is often standard in the queer community and agreed to it anyway. I always wanted us to get tested together, but they weren't into that. Eventually a local clinic was offering couples' testing, and I convinced them we should go. When the counselor arrived with our preliminary results, she said they came back different—I had tested positive. My stomach dropped. I had no job, no health insurance and no savings. I thought, *What's going to happen to me?*

At the time, you had to wait three weeks for conclusive results to come in. I spent them in purgatory, praying the test had been wrong. When I went back in, the doctor immediately started discussing treatment options. As he spoke, his words blurred together—I thought my brain was going to explode. He had still never even said the words: *You are HIV positive.*

After I left that day, I went through every stage of grief. I didn't really know how to talk about it at first and felt really alone. My partner was there but was more focused on how *they* were feeling and what *they* needed rather than what I needed. More than once, I created an out for them to jump ship, and our relationship ended within a year. At the time, I was interning at a youth center that helped young queer folks who were experiencing homelessness; many of them had HIV. I started having nightmares that I had become the populations I was serving, and I'd wake up feeling guilty because I knew so many brave people were already living through that.

I tried to resolve my feelings by being very public about my status—I'm still not entirely sure why. My family and friends were supportive, and after speaking with them, I started to post about it on Facebook. Since so much of my work is bound to HIV treatment and prevention, I thought I was creating a safe space for other people to share their struggles—trauma and tragedies have the power to bring people together. But broadcasting my status that early made it harder for me to cope.

I have a history of putting the needs of others before my own. I grew up in a house with two brothers who had developmental disabilities and a mother with a learning disability, plus other mental health issues. Helping them always came first. I learned that by taking care of others and making them happy, I had a role to play—but that also let me avoid confronting my own needs.

By being so public about my HIV status on social media, I felt I had to appear okay to others—if I looked like I was okay, I thought, everyone around me would feel okay with it. But I wasn't okay yet.

The first HIV medication I took had terrible side effects. If I wasn't lying down, I would get really dizzy and nauseated. My doctor recommended I take it in the evening so sleep would diminish the symptoms, but they lingered well into the next afternoon. I often hosted performances in the evenings, so my meds hindered my ability to work. It was debilitating, and I became depressed. My doctor wanted me to be undetectable before changing my pill, but I was ready to stop taking medication altogether—until Pancakes arrived.

One evening, I was hosting a show when I had to leave early because the side effects became unbearable. When I finally got home after the brutal hour-long trip on public transit, I was overwhelmed with guilt for having left something I produced. The next morning, I started to slip into depression. I kept thinking, *Is this the future? Do I have to give up doing work I love because of my health?* But then Pancakes stood up in bed, started wagging her tail and brought me a ball to play. It may sound like a small thing, but it shifted my focus from what I might be losing to what I had in front of me. Mental health might be the hardest part of an HIV diagnosis, and that little distraction stopped me from falling into a dark place.

I've learned a lot since then about how to take care of myself and how to *talk* about taking care of myself. My responsibility to Pancakes—to get up each morning to feed and walk her—provided the incentive to keep going until I could switch to a pill with fewer side effects. As of this writing, the performance project I feared I'd have to give up, "Queer, Ill and OK," is in its seventh year. Every night, I take my pill after my evening walk with Pancakes. When I prepare her food in the morning, I take my vitamins and make healthy meals for myself. When I'm sad, she sits in front of me and puts her head against mine. And in bed, she curls up in the crook of my arm. I see her adorable face looking back at me and think to myself, *Whatever is going on is not that bad.*

It has always been easier for me to be responsible if I have to do it for someone else. Caring for Pancakes showed me I had been shaping so much of my life based on what I thought other people needed, when I really should have been thinking about what I needed. In the first year after my diagnosis, Pancakes alleviated the pressure to keep it together in front of others, to let go of all of the expectations I put on myself. Pancakes didn't care about some public persona; she was going to be there no matter what. With her, I didn't have to pretend. She provided the unconditional love I could not give myself and that I struggled to ask for or find in others. She helped me build a healthier relationship with myself when I really needed it.

When I tell this story, people often say that Pancakes' arriving at the bus stop that October night was a sign. To me, it really doesn't matter whether it was the universe or god intentionally bringing me something or if it was just a matter of circumstance. All that's really important is that it happened. Because Pancakes came into my life, a lot of other good things followed. Whether or not it was divine, it was a gift all the same.

Owning My Story

AMADOR & BELLA

met Bella four years ago, when a friend of mine called me to clean the home of one of her clients. When I stepped in the door, this furry little Pomeranian appeared. It was Bella, and she was just a few months old. As soon as she saw me, she started running and jumping around. She followed me all over the house as I cleaned, and when it was time for me to leave, she jumped inside my supplies bag. When the woman who owned that house eventually had to move into a nursing home, she couldn't take her dogs with her. She remembered me and told my friend she wanted me to have Bella.

From the moment I brought her home, Bella wouldn't leave my side. Little did I know that a year later, Bella's unwavering presence would save my life.

At the time, I was working two jobs. I ran the cleaning service during the day, and I worked at a nursing home overnight, so I wasn't home a lot. One evening I wasn't feeling well—I had a high fever and my body ached (I was likely seroconverting without realizing it)—and I left work early to go home. When I got there, my partner of three years had people over to hook up—apparently this had been going on for a while. I felt like I had walked into a nightmare.

That was when everything started to fall apart. He and I broke up but stayed in the apartment for a couple weeks while we tried to find new living situations, and it was toxic. When we fought, he often became violent, and eventually the neighbors complained to the landlord. An eviction notice came soon after.

I knew we had nowhere to go. My mother suffers from depression and bipolar disorder, and she was living in a facility that didn't allow her to have guests stay over. I didn't want to burden my friends and their families with taking in both me and my dog. As I packed what I could into the car, I broke down crying—I felt like nobody wanted me or wanted to deal with me. In that moment, Bella placed her paw on top of my hand and looked at me. I knew then everything was going to be okay. No one else mattered—I would rather be with my dog living on the streets than be anywhere else without her.

We spent the next six months living in my car. Bella didn't mind; she's so tiny she could stay anywhere. I tried to keep us near parks where I could walk her. My mom helped us buy food, and once winter arrived, she gave us a place to warm up during the day. We were making it work, but I started getting sicker. Ordinarily, I'm a healthy person. I rarely get sick, let alone stay sick for weeks on end. I knew something wasn't right.

Finally, I went to the clinic and got tested. When the doctor told me I was HIV positive, l sat in the parking lot for two hours wondering how I was going to go on, and I contemplated suicide. What stopped me was Bella. It may sound ridiculous, but I pictured her not knowing what happened to me and it broke my heart. No one could take care of her the way I could, and to take care of her, I needed to be healthy.

I put my cleaning business on hold for a while and found an organization in Chicago where I could get help. When they found out I was living in my car, they helped Bella and me find a home. They helped me pay for dog food and certify Bella as a service animal. The combined stresses of my abusive relationship, childhood trauma and homelessness started triggering seizures. I trained Bella to be able to sense when I'm about to have one, and she barks and tugs at me to sit so I won't fall and get hurt.

Things started to get brighter. I developed a routine to pair taking my medication with Bella's walks, and we spent more time outside together, so we'd both get exercise. I could feel myself growing stronger physically and mentally each day. When a close family member outed me as HIV positive to the rest of my family, rumors quickly started to spread among my relatives and I felt like I was slipping backwards. Rather than crumble, I decided in that moment that I would be the one to tell my story moving forward. Through a series of homemade documentaries, I finally put the narrative back in my hands and was able to speak openly about my diagnosis and all that I've been through.

Of course, there are people on social media and dating apps who say I should have just kept my story to myself. There is still a lot of stigma around HIV even within the gay community, especially when it comes to dating. I want to meet someone and settle down, but I am surprised by how often I am met with fear when I disclose my status. I once was on a date and after I told the guy I was poz, he said, "This is too much for me." Then he got up and went home. In moments like these, I've felt discouraged. There are times I've questioned my decision to be so forthright with my story and my status and I've wondered whether it will get better. But at the end of the day, I believe in the power of using my voice to educate others.

Where I grew up, there isn't much support or education around HIV. I've seen so many kids like me in the waiting room at the clinic all alone. I recognize the look on their faces and the feelings behind their eyes—I want to help, especially among the Latino community, where people are afraid because they don't speak English or because they don't have documents. They are out there spreading and contracting the virus without knowing it because they're simply too afraid to ask for help. I've started collecting pamphlets and protection from the clinic to distribute outside clubs, and most

When Dogs Heal

recently I applied for a program to become a caseworker so I can pay it forward. Change starts within ourselves. I figure if I can change even just my own attitude, it helps move the needle.

Now that I have HIV, I take my life more seriously; I value what I have more. A lot of that has to do with Bella. I've learned from her to be faithful to those who stand by you through good and bad and that there's immense power in unconditional love. If I hadn't had Bella when I was diagnosed, I would probably be locked up in a mental institution or dead. I wouldn't be here talking to you.

These days, I am thankful for what I experienced and for who I am because of it. On the days when I feel down, I just think of Bella and those hopeless feelings go away. When I'm depressed or crying, she cuddles with me and licks my face or barks until I get up, go outside and enjoy the day. She keeps me on my toes. In the years since my diagnosis and that low point in the parking lot, it's clear that not only will no one care for Bella the way I do—but no one will take care of me the way that she can. I am reminded of that every time I look into her eyes.

A Passion for Life

GARY & HARRY

have been on permanent disability since 1995, when my HIV condition progressed to full-blown AIDS. After years of battling depression and anxiety that came with being a long-term survivor, my doctor suggested a companion dog might be good for me. He even offered to write me a note, prescribing a service dog, since my building didn't allow pets. I considered it—I love dogs—but didn't act on it for years.

Then, in 2005, I started seeing this adorable dog named Harry tied to parking meters outside of the laundromats and cafes in my neighborhood. Every time I saw him, I couldn't help but stop to play. Harry was just a puppy then, and he took to me immediately. It got to the point that my friend would call me whenever she had a Harry sighting, and I'd go out of my way to pet him for a little while. One night, I saw him outside a bar—the wind was cold blowing over the ocean and Harry was shivering. I picked him up, put him under my coat, held him next to my body and thought, *Where in the world is his owner?*

When I finally ran into the guy who I thought was his owner, I stopped to tell him he had the cutest dog I'd ever seen. Brad, it turned out, was a volunteer from Wonder Dog Rescue and was fostering Harry while he looked for a forever home. I remembered then what my doctor had said and thought that maybe I could have this dog Harry.

I hadn't known anyone who was HIV positive until I moved to San Francisco in 1987. The medical community had recently stated likely causes—unprotected sex, intravenous drug use—which seemed preventable, so I wasn't worried. Then in 1988, I had a kidney stone attack. During treatment, the doctor told me I was HIV positive. There I was thinking I'd be able to avoid it, and I was already positive.

I had just started my 401(k). I went to the bank to cash it out, and when I tried to apply for life insurance, I was redlined because of my zip code. I was, and still am, living in San Francisco's Castro District where AIDS was increasingly visible. Young guys, my age, were wasting away, moving through the streets with canes or in wheelchairs. I lost more than five hundred friends to AIDS-related illnesses, including my two best friends. After a while, I just quit counting. Like many survivors, I have PTSD from years spent wondering what was keeping me alive when everyone else around me was dying.

At the time, we thought doctors would solve the problem quickly—we'd have a drug for it in no time. Instead, the government didn't respond. Members of ACT UP and other activist groups put their lives on the line—doing work that benefited not just people suffering from HIV/AIDS but people with other life-threatening illnesses—and I cycled through almost every medication in the book.

I started on AZT in 1995; that was the hardest. As the virus mutated and the drug stopped working, I came down with thrush in my mouth, red bumps on my skin, neuropathy and lost 15 percent of my body weight. For a while, I was taking twenty-four pills a day and I'd spend hours staring at them scattered across my coffee table, trying to time them right. I was thankful to have medication, but sometimes I got tired of taking the damn things. I got tired of the fear that if I missed a dose and the virus mutated again, there'd be nothing left for me to take. Often, I'd leave my doctor's office wondering, *How long can I keep this up?*

My doctor, a gay man and pioneer in HIV/AIDS research, was my lifeline. I credit him for keeping me alive. I also found an LGBTQ-friendly, New Age ministry that was nicknamed Disco Church, because it drew five hundred people on a Sunday afternoon and kicked off with dance music, followed by a meditation. They hosted talks on self-healing that changed the way I coped with my diagnosis. I learned to use visualization, affirmations, meditation and the law of attraction. When I worried about things like access to medication, I reminded myself that you do not heal through fear; you heal through compassion and having a passion for life. That's why even when I don't feel well, I do activism and fundraising work to help others. I have raised a million dollars in my life for AIDS-related charities and have no plans to stop.

I knew a lot of survivors who were depressed and felt like their lives were over. I focused on living instead. And Harry helped.

Almost immediately after I adopted Harry from Wonder Dog Rescue, I felt a greater responsibility to stay alive and stay healthy. I exercised and got fresh air whether I wanted to or not, because Harry needed me to. If I was depressed, Harry was affected by my mood, so I didn't let myself stay low. It can be hard when you live alone and there's no one to ask if you're okay or to tell you a joke. But Harry would come along and throw a toy in the air and then look at me like, Well, are you going to get it? And I'd lose it. He knew how to make me and everyone around me laugh.

My friend Deana took Harry to work with her at a retail shop that raised money for HIV/AIDS. He wore an employee name tag on his collar and greeted customers, and she watched as people came in giggling and smiling. When we'd be driving and come to a stoplight, I'd look over to find a car full of people laughing and waving at Harry, whose face was out the window, tongue flapping like crazy.

He was a great companion. I think a lot of long-term HIV survivors give up on relationships. Your body changes as you age, and we got sick in our twenties or thirties, our prime earning years. Between the financial, physical and emotional effects, it can feel like you're not the most sought-after partner. Having a dog fills that void. A dog loves you unconditionally. If you're shy, or you're not feeling well, or you don't like how you look, your dog doesn't care. And when you take him out for a walk, he forces you to interact with people and smile.

I never felt alone when Harry was with me. At night, we'd lie nose to nose and I'd say, "I just love you." He would look into my eyes without blinking, and there was this complete trust that we would take care of each other always.

Harry passed away in 2016. In the last year of his life, there were moments when I could tell he didn't feel well; his energy was different. It turned out he had a tumor on his spleen. When I took him to the vet, the tumor erupted. It would have required surgery, a transfusion and a really difficult recovery, and before I could make a decision, he passed on his own.

I believe people come into our lives for a reason, and dogs do too. Before I knew that Harry needed a home, there were so many times I would pass him on the street and think, what a coincidence that I keep running into this same, sweet dog. Of course, it wasn't a coincidence that Harry showed up in my life when I needed him most. It was destiny.

When I lost Harry, my friends knew I was not in a good way. A few said, "Get out there, Gary. Another dog needs rescuing," but I couldn't. It was like losing my child. I believe souls can come back in different bodies, so the afternoon Harry passed I whispered to him, "If you had a good time and want to come back, find a way to let me know it's you."

It was a year after his passing before I started to look at dog rescue sites. It seemed like every six months I would write to one and get my hopes up, and it wouldn't work out. I finally rescued another dog last August. I saw her online and picked her up from Fresno. Her name is Tater, like tater tots. Whenever people who knew Harry meet Tater they say, "Oh my god, she reminds me so much of Harry!" She has his same temperament and mannerisms, even though she's a blond, long-haired dachshund. I laugh and think, *Well, Harry came back as a blond this time.*

There's a reason we have emotional support animals. Research shows animals can help lower blood pressure and cholesterol levels, cure loneliness, increase exercise, improve your social life. Pet owners with AIDS are less likely to be depressed than nonowners. Kids who grow up with cats and dogs have fewer allergies and asthma, stronger immune systems and learn greater responsibility. And for me: Fourteen years later, I am on four pills twice a day and I finally got my viral load undetectable.

A dog's energy lifts us to a higher place—it's that simple. Dogs don't worry about their futures or their medications. They go through life enjoying their Kibbles 'n Bits. When they're thirsty they drink, when they have to pee they let you know, and when they want to play with another dog, they go for it. No one has a greater passion for life than a dog. Maybe we should take a cue.

How to Stop Loneliness

FELECIA, GYPSY ROSE LEE & SIMON

Being a transsexual woman, I've had a very lonely life.

To stay numb to the loneliness, I became deeply involved with my community, constantly volunteering and doing activist work for the past forty years.

In 1987, I was living in San Jose and volunteering at a local HIV/AIDS agency. At the time, I never thought I would be just like the people I was helping, even though I never used protection with sexual partners. I thought that if my partners were sick, they would have told me. But it just didn't happen like that.

One day, while being trained on HIV/AIDS prevention at work, I found out I was HIV positive. At first it was a surprise, but then the surprise disappeared into the California winds. It was one more thing that made me different, and I realized that deep down I always thought I deserved my diagnosis, because who I am is against God's law. I thought I deserved that punishment.

No matter how much I worked, I started to feel more and more lonely, so I pushed my way out of San Jose and moved up to San Francisco. And there I found a way to help me not feel so lonely: Sammy.

Sammy was a shelter dog that I rescued. When I would come home, the first thing I would see was Sammy all excited to greet me. I had never experienced that before in my life—and it felt so good. As time went on, I felt like Sammy was getting lonely because he spent so much time at home by himself while I was busy at work. So I got Shadow, a bichon, and none of us were lonely for a very long time. It was the first time in my life that I felt unconditional love.

I've never felt worthy or valuable as a human being. The stigma of being transsexual and HIV positive has always made me feel like trash. My children—my dogs, Shadow and Sammy—changed all that, and I couldn't imagine living without them.

When they died, the loneliness they had kept at bay came rushing back in. I took time to mourn them and was hesitant to get another dog. But after some time, I stumbled across a dog on Craigslist and it felt right. That's how I got Gypsy Rose Lee, my little girl. Getting Gypsy Rose Lee gave me purpose and strength again. And just like before, I felt I had to get her someone to make her feel less lonely, which is how I got Simon.

What I've learned throughout my life is that while I struggle to feel loved and supported by the people around me, I can always rely on my dogs, no matter what. They are the main reason I am alive today. Since I became positive, even with my activist work, my dogs are the real motivation for me to get up in the morning and to go out and do things. It is my responsibility as a mother and a dog owner to make sure that Gypsy Rose Lee and Simon have the quality of life they deserve, and to do that, I've learned that I too have to have a good quality of life.

Had I not had my dogs, all of them, I would have died a long time ago from loneliness. To this day, when I open the door and they are all there wagging their tails, I am overwhelmed by a feeling I don't think a human can give me. And when I am sick—which seems to be happening more and more frequently these days—my dogs are there to help me heal.

My Rock

TREMAINE, ROCKY BALBOA & MADAM RUSSIA

Before I got Rocky, my life was at its lowest point and my HIV was spiraling out of control.

I was diagnosed a few years prior, at the age of seventeen. Right off the bat I hated the side effects of the medications, so I quickly stopped taking them. My health got worse soon after that. I got an opportunistic infection and became really sick.

Looking back, I realize that choosing to go off meds wasn't so much about the side effects. It was about me not loving myself after learning I was positive. I wasn't taking care of myself, and my body was falling apart. At the time I was living in Atlanta with my mom, who was also going through a lot of personal stuff, so my life felt like a constant state of negativity—until I met Rocky.

I remember that day; looking into his eyes I could see his quiet strength. It was a strength I really connected to and desperately needed in my life. When I took Rocky home, I thought about all the stuff going on in my life and said, "If you can't turn your life around for yourself, then you have to do it for Rocky."

That day he became my rock. My constant companion. I felt like I couldn't improve things while living in Atlanta, so I moved to New York City. With Rocky by my side, I found my footing in a new city and a new home, and all the negativity I had been feeling began to fade away. I began making room for positive things in my life, and that's when we met Madam Russia.

Even though Rocky and I were doing fine on our own, I knew that he too needed a companion. Thinking about all of this now, I honestly don't know what life would be without him. I don't know if I ever would have had the courage or strength to leave Atlanta. And ultimately, I don't know if I ever would have started prioritizing my health and loving myself.

Today loving myself looks like taking medication to make sure that my immune system is functioning at its best. Loving myself means surrounding myself with supportive people and environments that motivate and challenge me to be the best that I can be. And while that may be a lifelong process, I have my life back because of my rock, my Rocky.

My Reassurance

COLEMAN & DODO

When Dodo was a puppy, she belonged to a different family. Her owners had another dog that didn't take well to the new addition, and they needed to find Dodo a new home. My parents got wind of it and wanted to bring her home. I thought they were crazy. At the time, we had a much older dog who needed a lot of care.

"A puppy is so much work," I said. "Why would you get another dog right now?"

I was twenty-two, fresh out of college, and working from 7 a.m. to 6:30 p.m. at a job I hated. After a particularly rough day at work, I came home exhausted to find this adorable little puppy running toward me from across the house. She jumped into my lap, and instantly I fell in love. We had to keep her.

For the first few months, Dodo had this habit of running away whenever we'd open the door. I would chase her around the neighborhood for hours, trying to get her safely inside. It was as if she was afraid of something, maybe from a traumatic experience she had before we got her. Her rebellion went on for months, until finally one night she went down a neighbor's dead-end driveway. She was fenced in, and I cornered her. Once she saw she couldn't get away from me, it was like something clicked in her head. She let me pick her up and take her back inside, and she never tried to run away again. The experience bonded us. From then on, we were exceptionally close.

I was diagnosed with HIV five years ago. After a monthlong battle with a nasty sore throat, I made an appointment with an ear, nose and throat doctor. He kept pushing to prescribe me heartburn medication, despite me telling him I don't suffer from heartburn. The experience left a bad taste in my mouth. Ordinarily, I trust doctors, but I knew something wasn't right. When I found a new doctor—a gay doctor who has a lot of gay patients—the first thing he did was test me for HIV.

It was really hard to hear the words: "You are HIV positive." There's a connotation to them, and it took some time for me to accept my diagnosis. At first, I became angry—I don't know who gave it to me, and I hadn't slept with many people. I'm lucky we caught it and that it was not 1992, but my diagnosis still came with challenges.

Because I'd had the virus for several months before we caught it, I had a major problem with my insurance. My company's health plan had outsourced its prescription drug program to a company in Michigan that excluded coverage for any type of HIV or AIDS medication. My doctor was baffled; he'd never seen anything like it before. I thought, *Well, what the hell does that mean? What do I do now?*

I hadn't even come to terms with my own feelings about it yet, and I had to call my company's HR department and disclose to them that I now had HIV. I called the insurance company essentially begging for coverage—and all of that took my diagnosis from challenging to stressful to shameful.

While she probably didn't know I had HIV specifically, Dodo sensed something was wrong. As I felt repeatedly frustrated and dehumanized by my insurer, I struggled to trust others. But Dodo met me with love and joy and constant support. It became enough to know that when I'd come home, that little fur ball would be waiting for me—she gave me something to look forward to.

It took me several months to be able to start consistent treatment, which compounded my sense of fear and frustration for a while, but things eventually leveled out. I had thought that sort of stigma from health-care providers was ancient history, but I've learned the hard way that HIV stigma is alive and well.

The truth is, I think many of us still struggle with stigma. Months before my own diagnosis, my roommate tested positive and I was a little insensitive. I was young and lacked perspective, plus this was before PrEP, which has changed the game a bit. But I also think the gay community still hasn't fully come to terms with this virus and how to be open about it without judgment. I still meet guys who don't know about PrEP or who have ghosted me once I've told them I was positive, leaving me to question whether it was me or the HIV. I once met a guy at a bar and after we kissed, I disclosed my status to him. He messaged me the next day to say that I "shouldn't be kissing anyone"—and he was in medical school! I am a real person with real feelings. When that's how people react, it makes me want to talk about it even less. The reality is, secrecy and shame are what keep this disease alive.

Even though I'm open about my status in dating and socially, my family still doesn't know. I'm out with them about my sexuality, but they tend to be dramatic and self-involved and don't understand gay culture. I've decided it is easier, for now, to keep that part of my life separate from them.

Also, things are pretty grim with my family these days. My dad has terminal leukemia, and my mom recently had a hip replacement. Even though Dodo is not that young—she's twelve, which is old for a boxer—she brings a lightness that makes it all a bit easier to handle. She's affectionate and being with her is comforting. Sometimes I like to sit on the porch steps by myself, and she'll sit next to me and rest her head in my lap; I take her collar off and scratch under her neck. In those moments, I can say anything and be my full self. Dodo doesn't care about cultural constraints or stigma, and she is always happy to see me. And it's not that I don't get that from my family or friends, but with dogs there are no strings attached or conditions. With Dodo, everything is simpler.

Dodo came into my life just as I was starting to define myself as an adult and establish my place in the world. As I've gotten older, relationships with family and friends have changed, but my relationship with Dodo has never wavered. She has always been an invaluable source of positivity in my life. Every time I walk through that door, she howls with excitement just to see me—what could be more reassuring than that?

The Princess Who Saved Us

BERT, KEILA & DAVID

My partner was a recovering addict when he moved to Los Angeles to live with me. We battled his addiction for a while together, but it just wasn't working. On top of living with AIDS, he simply couldn't seem to get sober. David wanted a dog so badly that one day I remember telling him, "If you stay sober for a year, we can get a dog." And that finally did the trick.

Right before he hit the one-year mark, I took him to the Beverly Center one day with two of our friends. There was a boxer puppy there that I was considering buying him, but he had no idea. When we arrived at the pet store in the mall, I showed him the puppy and told him to pet her. As they played, I remember watching and feeling like this was a match made in heaven, and that even though he had previously told me he wanted a male boxer, he was already in love with this female and it just felt right. That's how we got Keila.

The night we brought Keila home I saw David change. A payoff for all the work he had done the past year to get and stay sober. For the rest of David's life he was a stay-at-home dad, and Keila was with him 24/7. They would go everywhere together, which made David so happy. And seeing him happy made me happy. Without her, I don't think he would have ever stayed sober or lived as long as he did with his diagnosis. We felt that happiness for so many years. All the way until David died on October 25, 1995, just seventeen days after his fortieth birthday.

He was buried in Massachusetts and Keila was at the funeral, like everyone knew she would be. I remember that day so well. She walked up to the casket and just stared at him. After that day, I became a single dad and Keila and I comforted each other with David gone. My life was half as happy, just like hers.

When Keila died, I had her cremated and sprinkled the ashes over David's grave. That day was horrible because her dying was like reliving David dying all over again. There is a picture of them together on his tombstone, and I visit them as often as I can, remembering how happy our lives became once she was there. And I always remember that this dog is what made his life the happiest it had ever been, through the addictions and being diagnosed with AIDS. Knowing they are now forever together somehow makes me happy and pushes me through that pain.

Since they died, I have not had another dog or partner, but I am happy still. And lately, I've been thinking of getting another boxer, a female, and maybe trying dating once again. Maybe.

My Daily Reminder

BRAD & SOOKIE

tested positive in 2000. I was twenty years old.

It was my first time in rehab, and I was in a private office—terrified—after doing my intake, which included a mandatory HIV test. When they told me I was positive, I fell off my chair, hit my head and passed out. I woke up in a hospital bed sometime later, where the rehab staff told me once again about my new diagnosis. All I remember is that I had a terrible headache and none of it seemed real.

The only thing I knew back then about HIV was that people were dying, and I was convinced that I'd be dead in six months. I decided that if I was going to die, I wanted to go out with a bang, and after being released from rehab I proceeded to spend the next eight years high on crystal meth. During that time, I was in and out of hospitals and jails, living on the streets and doing sex work. I was an addict, but somehow I stayed alive for quite some time. Well, much more time than anyone expected.

There is that turning point that rehab programs call "a moment of clarity." It's when you finally decide you want to get clean. Mine happened during my last stint in jail. It finally hit me that if I wasn't going to die from the drugs, I would certainly spend the rest of my life in jail, and I just couldn't let that happen. As soon as I walked out of that jail, I began my sober journey, but it wasn't easy. That's why I got Sookie.

Just before Sookie came into my life, my boyfriend and I were living in an apartment above a garage with only a mattress on the floor and an old TV. We were so broke that we ate ramen noodles for every meal. At the time, I needed something positive in my life because my boyfriend was still getting high while I fought to stay sober. One evening I went onto Craigslist and found an ad for puppies. I decided to reach out.

The woman who placed the ad called me that night and told me that she lived an hour and a half north of our apartment. She said that her neighbor had recently passed away and she was selling their animals to help make money for the family. Three days later, she showed up at my house with her husband, three children and two puppies.

When they arrived, I told them my story: how I had been on my own since my parents had kicked me out at age fifteen for being gay, how I was struggling with addiction and my HIV diagnosis, how I needed something to help me get out of bed and keep me on the right track. As we spoke, little Sookie jumped into my lap and I said, "I think she could help me."

Since then, Sookie has helped me in ways I could have never imagined. There have been times I've thought about getting high, and she's there to remind me that I can't risk going back to drugs—not just for myself, but for her too. I know I couldn't have stayed sober for this long without her because she was the first thing in my life to show me unconditional love. The joy and comfort she brings makes me so grateful that I didn't end my life with a bang so many years ago. Instead, I came to life with a bark and she reminds me of that every day.

The Love I Deserved

LYNNEA & COCONUT

found out I was HIV positive when I was seven. For months I had been going with my mom to the doctor, getting my blood drawn and taking medicine I didn't like. I assumed it was normal, but my older sister kept asking questions about it. Finally, she confronted our mom and said, *You're not doing it to the rest of us, so what's going on?*

That's when my mom gave in and told her. I had been playing in the yard, and when I came inside to ask my sister to join me, the first thing she did was tell me that I was HIV positive—even though our mom made her promise not to. I was devastated. I ran into the kitchen crying to my mom, *Why didn't you tell me I was dying?*

It was 1992, and all I knew about HIV was what I heard in the news. Magic Johnson had retired from basketball because he'd been diagnosed with HIV (a death sentence at the time), and Ryan White had been kicked out of school for going public with his own HIV diagnosis. Back then HIV only meant AIDS, and it meant you were dying.

My mom knelt down and told me that even though I had HIV, I wasn't dying. She told me she had AIDS, which was a little worse but the same germ. I still had to go to school, she said, and I had to keep living my life. She was making sure I had everything I needed, and as long as I saw her getting up each day, then I would too, because she was worse off than me. My mother is still alive and healthy today, and I think about that often.

Because of what happened with Ryan White, my mom told me not to tell kids at school about my status. But in fourth grade, a girl who I thought was my friend told me a secret of hers, so I told her mine. She immediately backed away and said, *My mom says that's for gay people, and you're gonna die.* That was the last time I ever talked to that girl. I went from thinking I had a friend to thinking this person hated me for something I couldn't change about myself. My mom found a support group for me, so I could spend time with kids who were going through what I was going through, but I sometimes felt like I had two separate lives.

In my early twenties I came out to some people, but many couldn't get past their own biases. From that point on, I assumed people wouldn't be accepting of my status. I avoided expressing interest in friendships and romantic relationships. If someone pursued me, I didn't pick the right partner because I mistook acceptance for love. For ten years I struggled to get out of an abusive relationship because I believed that because of my diagnosis, I should be grateful—lucky, even—to have anyone at all. I thought, *I'm HIV-positive; who would want to be with me?*

Then I got Coconut, who changed all of that.

Coconut was an accident. A friend of mine asked me to help her find a dog, so I went on Craigslist and found Coconut. When I picked him up, there was an immediate bond between us. He spent the entire forty-minute drive back home faithfully sitting on my shoulder. He turned out to be a little too calm for my friend, who had multiple young children and wanted a more spirited dog they could run around with. Newly pregnant and living in an apartment by myself, I was hesitant to keep him. I didn't think I had the time or energy for a dog, but as soon as I brought him home, it felt as if he already belonged there.

There's a joke someone once told me: If you want to know who loves you most, lock your spouse and your dog in the trunk of a car for an hour. When you open it, see which one is more excited to see you. It sounds silly maybe, but that's how I started looking at my relationships—that this person should love me on my worst days.

During the pregnancy, I had terrible morning sickness. There were days I didn't want to get out of bed, days when my growing belly felt so heavy on my bones that with every step I buckled in pain. Sometimes I would just sit on the floor for hours, unable to get up. When that happened, Coconut would come over and curl up in my lap, or he would jump up and lick me, giving me the spark of energy I needed to go on. His love and affection were constant and refreshing. Eventually I realized, if I am good enough for this dog, how could I not be good enough for my boyfriend?

Coconut showed me that I deserved more out of a partner—not just for me but for the baby girl growing inside of me. Soon my daughter would be looking at me as the example of who she's supposed to be. I would be responsible for showing her what a healthy relationship is. I watched my mom go through abusive relationships when I was young, and I decided that I wasn't going to perpetuate that cycle anymore. We deserved better.

A few months after getting Coconut, I finally cut ties with my daughter's father. I stopped catering to him when he came over, and eventually he stopped coming. Being by myself felt really lonely at times. I cried a lot over what might come of my life after having a child. But Coconut made it better just by being there. He wouldn't let me sit around feeling depressed. Instead, he became my practice baby. I tended to him when he needed hugs or to be fed or to go out. Not only did it force me to get up and move around, it helped me build confidence in becoming a mother. And if there wasn't anything to do, Coconut would start chasing his tail and give me something to laugh about.

Lately, I've found myself not hiding in silence anymore. I no longer look at HIV as something negative in my life or as a reason to push people away. I've seen the bad—

I've been with the bad—my relationship with Coconut during my pregnancy helped me see that I am worth more and to take the leap I needed to not compromise on that. Instead of looking for a person who's okay with my status, I look now for a person I can be happy with. Coconut has shown me I can be loved by another living thing—that I deserve a love that doesn't hurt.

My Main Focus

BRYAN & TACO

was diagnosed with HIV on August 15, 2009—the first day of the worst year of my life.

I had been in a relationship for five years when a routine HIV test came back positive. There was no way that I could have contracted the virus other than through my partner, John. When I confronted him and he refused to get tested, it was clear that I couldn't trust him anymore. About a month after I moved out of our apartment, he and I went out for dinner to discuss the idea of reconciling. "Unless I'm able to trust you," I said, "it's not going to happen. First and foremost, you need to get tested."

For the rest of the night he was despondent and had stopped listening. When I dropped him off, there were tears in his eyes. The next morning his boss called me and said John hadn't shown up to work, which was unlike him. I called him several times, but he didn't answer. Finally, I drove to the apartment and the bedroom door was locked. I broke in and found John inside, barely breathing. He had taken seventy-nine Vicodin with two liters of vodka and aspirated.

I rushed him to the hospital, but he was in bad shape. In the emergency room, he flatlined three times before my eyes. It was horrible. John's dad flew into town, and the two of us monitored his progress. In six days, he never regained consciousness, and when the doctors ran an electroencephalogram (EEG), they told us John was brain-dead. We decided to stop life-sustaining measures, and he died on September 11.

In the month between my diagnosis and my partner's death, I hadn't thought once about how to handle my own health. After John's memorial, I finally sought out a medical provider and allowed myself to fall apart. With him gone, it was our two dogs—a beagle named Molly and a bichon frise named Reni (John's favorite breed was a bichon and mine was a beagle)—that kept me sane. They were excited to see me even when I couldn't bear to be around myself. I never had to put on a brave face for them, and they gave me stability when the rest of my life felt out of control.

When it was time to go back to work, I got a new job and buried myself in it. I didn't want to think about or feel anything. I had to hire a dog-walking service to take care of the dogs because I stayed at the office late every night. For two years, I used work to hide from my grief and the world.

When my company downsized, my role was eliminated. Suddenly I had lots of time on my hands—and that's when my demons came rushing in. I finally had to face everything that had happened since my HIV diagnosis. With the help of a wonderful counselor, I was able to acknowledge that, though I was a strong person, ignoring a problem isn't strength. I learned to accept my circumstances and to cherish moments I wouldn't have given a second thought to before—like going to the dog park. I started looking forward to those outings again. I met like-minded people and expanded my circle, while the dogs enjoyed a social life they'd been missing and deserved.

In 2016, Reni got cancer and we had to let him go. It was hard because he was John's favorite, so it kind of felt like I was letting go of another piece of John. After Reni passed, I didn't feel right having Molly by herself. I moved to Hawaii for a new job and asked my best friend to take her while I was gone. Her two sons fell in love with Molly, and I didn't have the heart to take her back.

I wasn't thinking about adopting a new dog when Taco came along. I was living with a man named Jimmy in Northern California, and one day while walking down the street we saw a tiny Maltese-Chihuahua running in the middle of a main thoroughfare. He couldn't have been more than two pounds. We were so worried for him that we ran into the street to scoop him up. A homeless man on the other side of the road started screaming at us to put the dog down, because it belonged to him. When we approached him, he had a larger adult dog too who had recently given birth to six puppies. The man said he'd sold the others, and this was the last one. We offered him money to take both dogs off the streets, but he was only willing to part with the puppy—for twenty bucks. I was short a few dollars, but we had just returned from Taco Bell; I gave the man a few tacos and all the cash I had, and that's how Taco got his name.

Just a couple months after we took Taco in, I came home from work to find Jimmy smoking crystal meth. It was my apartment—he wasn't on the lease—and I wasn't willing to have that sort of thing happening in my home. When I told him to pack his things, he shoved me into the refrigerator and—in trying to catch myself from hitting the floor—I broke my wrist. He then kicked over the garbage can, sending food all over the floor, and locked himself in the bathroom. I was trying to clean up the mess with my good hand when the police knocked on the door—my neighbor had reported a domestic disturbance. When they entered the apartment, my ex came out of the bathroom and told the police that I'd attacked him, and they immediately took me into custody.

I spent the night in the Santa Clara County jail freaking out over whether Taco was safe. He was so young at the time; he wasn't disciplined enough yet to be left alone. The district attorney dropped all the charges, and the next morning, when I walked through the door, I ran to Taco's crate—thank goodness he was there and unharmed.

Jimmy had never been violent towards me prior to that night, but based on his reaction when I confronted him about using, I wasn't going to risk it—not just for me but for Taco. He was just starting to learn what it meant to trust people, and I refused to put him in a position where he'd live in fear. The experience resurfaced feelings from the last time my trust was broken with John, and I knew it would have been difficult to get Jimmy out of my life if I stuck around. That morning, I quit my job, packed up the apartment and flew my mom out to San Francisco so we could drive my stuff back to Chicago together.

Now I am staying in my parents' spare room while I interview for a new job. I know that not everyone has parents who can help them the way mine have, and I'm grateful to have them and Taco with me as I make a fresh start.

Through this decade-long journey, I've realized that everybody craves purpose, to feel needed. After my HIV diagnosis, there were times when I felt the opposite—discarded or like I was wearing a scarlet letter—especially in the dating world. Those are the times when having an animal that needs and loves you no matter what is so critical. Reni and Molly provided me with that in the form of stability and routine at a time when I felt like I didn't even deserve to be alive, and today Taco is my comic relief—and that is just as meaningful.

He's only about six months old, so he's still learning. He wavers on potty training and wants to play round the clock. (We're at the 3 a.m. squeaky-toy-shoved-up-my-nose phase.) The other day, while he was chasing his toy, he fell down the stairs butt first and didn't even stop—he just kept running. He was so excited about his stupid toy, you know? It doesn't matter whether I'm away for five hours or five minutes, it's always the same reaction: "Oh my god I can't believe how much I missed you." It might be silly, but it feels good. When I'm with Taco, I am the real me—all the layers peel off. Taco keeps me finding joy in life's simple things. It's nice to finally be at a place in my life where that can be the main focus.

My Chosen Family

JOSEPH & GANESH

found out I was HIV positive during a routine visit with my doctor.

Finding out in that way wasn't heartbreaking but shocking. It knocked the wind out of me. I was going through a really tough time—my brother had recently passed and both of my parents were very sick. I was so busy taking care of all of them that I never even imagined I could be sick too.

I kept my status a secret for a while because I didn't want to burden my family—they were already dealing with so much. I hadn't yet come out as gay to anyone, and I knew telling them I was HIV positive would be a giveaway. I come from a conservative Muslim family; coming out just didn't seem like a possibility at the time.

Before I tested positive I didn't know anyone who had HIV, so I had no idea how I contracted the disease. None of my partners had said anything, so I just assumed I had nothing to worry about.

My father died next, and all I had left was my mother, who was battling Parkinson's disease. She was incredibly lonely without my father, so I decided to get her a dog after a coworker told me she was giving some away. That's how I met Ganesh.

The first day I met him there was this strong connection between us. I'd never had a dog before and had never felt something so powerful. It felt like we understood each other instantly. When I took Ganesh to meet my mother, he ended up favoring me and refusing to leave my side. My mother developed atrophy as a side effect from Parkinson's disease, and in the end she couldn't care for him anyway. It was just luck that Ganesh and I ended up together.

Having Ganesh was so special because he was the only one in the world that I could share everything with without any judgment or fear. He was the only thing around me that seemed to breathe life rather than illness. My mother died shortly afterwards, and all I felt was relief. She had been suffering for so long, and that was terrible to witness. The only sad part about all of this was that my entire family died without ever knowing the full me.

I've never been very social, but having to take Ganesh out for walks has made me more outgoing. Being active with him has helped me meet so many new people. I recently joined T2, which is the annual marathon to raise money for HIV/AIDS, and I've seen my life become fuller with new friends, new people just like me.

Since Ganesh, our family has grown and I've adopted two other puppies. No matter how many dogs come into our home, I will always be grateful that in the darkest moment of my life, when I had no one to lean on, Ganesh was there to listen, and he never left my side.

Embracing Life

SISTER LOTTI DA & SHINER

Before I got Shiner, I felt like death had a grip on my life. When I seroconverted, or became positive, I had a high-profile career. I helped create the cornerstone product for Thomson Reuters, the largest disseminator of financial information in the world. I've always been an overachiever and had invested so much in my career—work is what provided me with cultural, social and personal validity.

That all changed in the spring of 2000, when I came down with an awful case of pneumonia that I just couldn't kick. Though my routine HIV test a month earlier had come back negative and I had not engaged in any known high-risk behaviors, the pneumonia was a red flag. I retested two months later and it came back positive.

Fortunately, I was diagnosed at a time when I could start the antiretroviral cocktail right away. Had it been a decade earlier, I would have died months after being diagnosed, as many people did in the 1980s. That knowledge took a toll on my psyche; it kept me loyal to medications even as I suffered through hallucinations, persistent nausea and hives. I spent much of the next three years wasting away in bed, hopelessly comparing myself to the happy people rock climbing in pharmaceutical ads for the same drugs that were making me sick. I thought, *Just muscle through it; you should be grateful to have treatment at all.*

Eventually my health became so bad that I could no longer work. While losing my job impacted my finances, losing my career was emotionally debilitating and launched me into an identity crisis. Especially in New York, the first thing a person asks when they meet you is, "What do you do?" To go from having a dynamic, all-encompassing career to battling opportunistic infections and chronic diarrhea . . . I lost my sense of purpose.

Not only was I unable to work, I was not well enough to sit through a play or a party, so being sick became tremendously isolating. I stopped getting invitations to after-work cocktails. I became less desirable, less interesting in the "what-do-you-do" cocktail banter I'd been so entrenched in before. I found myself in the grocery store at 10 a.m. with the old men in my neighborhood—people I'd never noticed when I was waking up at 5 a.m. for conference calls and working sixty to eighty hours a week. I felt forgotten, thrust into an end-of-life experience before my time.

Many people advised me to keep my HIV diagnosis secret. Because it's an *acquired* illness, often the first question people ask is how you got it—looking for a way to assign blame to your health problems. But keeping my status a secret compounded the loneliness and sense of failure I had over not having protected myself. I felt broken. At a certain point, between the side effects of my meds, the isolation and the stigma, it became tempting to turn to recreational drugs to numb the pain and manufacture intimacies. As anyone who has struggled with addiction can tell you, it's a slippery slope (and an all-too-common experience for the newly diagnosed). I was no different.

In 2003, I got my first dog, Sawyer. My sister's dog had just had a litter of pups, and my family thought it might be good for me to take on the runt. That was the best decision of my life.

Sawyer pulled me out of the depression that came with my diagnosis. This was way before one could be *undetectable*, a term people use now to confer not being a danger to others. Back then, I believed that I was a pariah, that by simply being in contact with someone, I could put them in danger. Most of the physical intimacy in my life came from doctors and nurses taking my vitals. Yet Sawyer just wanted to be close to me. She loved me no matter what. Sawyer pulled me out of self-pity and forced me to interact with the life around me. As we walked through the park, I became aware of and grateful for the seasons. I noticed when certain birds came out and when the leaves started to change. She provided me with a sense of connection greater than just companionship.

Sawyer was diagnosed with breast cancer at almost the same time my grandmother had a stroke. My grandmother was everything to me. Growing up as a queer kid and ballet dancer in the suburbs of San Antonio, I didn't fit into the paradigms that most people, including much of my family, embraced. All of that was irrelevant when I was with my grandma. Her home was a sanctuary throughout my life and provided a sense of safety, which hadn't always been easy to come by. With her, there was never any judgment or a need to explain myself; there was simply an invitation to be and to be loved. Soon after her stroke I bought a new car so that I could care for my grandmother and take Sawyer along with me. I wasn't working at the time, and I dedicated my time and energy to caring for both of them. Together, my grandmother and Sawyer gave my life shape, meaning and direction. They gave me a reason to stay alive.

Within a year I lost both my grandmother and Sawyer, and soon after I also lost my mother. I'd become a sort of death doula—helping other people and myself come to terms with the end of life. Preparing for and confronting death is emotionally and physically exhausting. Once you're on the other side of it, all you want to do is rest and grieve. But the more you rest, the more tired you are, and at some point, you realize you are most likely within some cycle of depression. Without a means of stepping out, it can be really easy to stay mired in it.

The structure in my life soon began to crumble. When you have HIV, structure is necessary for adhering to your medication, so my health soon started to decline as well. I felt broken all over again. Who was I, if I was not the good son, the person who took care of his grandmother, who gave his dog four walks a day? The things that contributed to my old identity were no longer available to me. Grief and renewed isolation encouraged old demons, and nothing provides structure like the empty promises of addiction. Living in New York City, the club, bar and music scenes are saturated with opportunities to party,

When Dogs Heal

do drugs and drink—things that aren't conducive to staying healthy. I watched many older gentlemen struggle with HIV-positive identity issues and fall into that trap. To people of a certain age, the trauma of the early AIDS epidemic—when HIV was a death sentence—is deeply ingrained. Diagnosed, then treated with medications that made me feel awful and fatigued, it became appealing to use drugs that could make me feel alive and sexy—especially if I didn't have a reason to take care of myself.

Thank goodness for Shiner, because she became my reason. When Shiner came into my life, it was kismet. I was driving back from Texas when I heard about this little Labrador puppy that no one wanted because she'd been born with a condition that caused her eyelids to develop inside out. The breeder was looking to place her in a good home, with the caveat that she would need surgery down the line. (This photograph was taken a couple months before that surgery, which is why her eyes are red.) Both of us being broken, we found each other.

When you have someone that depends on you, your own well-being becomes intrinsically connected to theirs. If I was feeling crappy, I knew that a walk in the park would be good for us both. I needed that magic to pull me out of the mundane. It sounds corny, but a dog gives you something to live for—it really is that rudimentary.

Having Shiner helped me reconnect to my community, my neighborhood and myself. Having a puppy with boundless energy and who needed to be trained required me to be front and center, to focus on the present. When I bring her to the park, I meet other people and make friends with the owners of dogs she likes to play with. She helps me remain connected to a larger social culture in a way I couldn't have imagined.

Over the years, I've found a new antiretroviral medication regimen that I tolerate better. I still struggle with some of the same issues (which may never go away), but I have become invested in staying healthy and engaged in the world. Shiner lifted me out of the doldrums, helped me view life with a fresh perspective and challenged me to reevaluate my purpose. Though I've essentially had to retire early because of HIV-related illnesses, when I feel up to it, I volunteer within the queer community through the Sisters of Perpetual Indulgence—a charity organization and activist group that uses drag and religious imagery to promote human rights, respect for diversity and spiritual enlightenment (hence the outfit). On days when the side effects are overwhelming and waves of grief wash over me, Shiner's smile and wagging tail motivate me to get out of bed and embrace life. It's simply hard to feel bad when a dog is asking you to play.

Because of Shiner, I am happier and healthier. I seek out joy more readily. Every day, Shiner reminds me of life's most important lessons: that we are all a part of the same pack, sometimes the best way to learn is through play and everyone holds the same possibility for goodness.

Taking a Chance

MITCH & PEANUT

got my HIV diagnosis in 1992. I was twenty-five years old and in love with an amazing guy named Barry. Early on in our relationship, we had agreed to get tested. My results came back negative, and Barry said he'd been told the same. We were monogamous, so we decided to switch to unprotected sex.

About two years into our relationship, Barry's body started to wither and show symptoms that seemed consistent with HIV. I eventually decided to get tested again. When my results came back positive, I moved out because it was clear he'd been lying to me for three years. I realized that Barry had never actually gone in to get tested at the beginning of our relationship because he couldn't face the potential fallout.

As background, you have to remember that Barry and I fell in love at a time when HIV was extremely scary and taboo. With a lack of treatment options available, people didn't want to talk about or face their diagnoses. So even though I was initially angry with Barry, we stayed close as he got sicker. When he was moved to the hospital, I visited often and made sure he was trying to get better. I was the only person he ever asked for by name, and he refused certain treatments unless I was there. I hit some unfortunate hurdles with his parents, but in his last days I got the opportunity to say goodbye and let him know I was there, which helped me get some closure.

And then my life went on. The doctors told me I had five years to live, but I basically told myself, "Nope. This isn't how I'm going down." I refused to let HIV kill me.

When I met Peanut, I was absolutely *not* looking for a dog. By then, it was the early 2000s. I was a thirty-eight-year-old gay dude who worked a lot, socialized a lot and liked being able to come and go as he pleased. Peanut belonged to my then boyfriend's sister and her family. From the moment I met this dog, I had a soft spot for her—she was sweet and loving and so affectionate that she immediately curled up into my lap.

My boyfriend's family believed that dogs belonged outside, even though their Northern California winters could get as cold as twenty degrees Fahrenheit. When February came, I convinced them to at least put Peanut in the garage with a bed to keep her out of the elements. His sister called me the next day to say her husband was pissed off because Peanut went to the bathroom in the garage, and she didn't know what to do. "Bring her to me," I said, and the next day I had a dog.

The moment I brought Peanut home, everything changed. She showed me what was missing from my life. My family isn't close, so I hadn't realized how important that sense of intimacy and commitment was to me. She forced me to consider being more than just a dude who goes out and has fun with his friends. With Peanut, I had a purpose.

I realized the real power in that in 2006, when I almost died from septic MRSA, a type of staph infection. It was easily the most pain I've felt in my life, and I pulled through largely because of Peanut. My boyfriend used to sneak her into the hospital in a bowling bag, and she would fall asleep on my shoulder. The nurses never batted an eye about having her in there with me. Though my survival was more or less in the doctor's hands, I believe that a positive mindset, and the support of friends and family, can have a profound impact on our health. Knowing I had Peanut waiting for me, needing me, made me fight harder to get better.

The following Thanksgiving, Peanut and I were out for a walk when we noticed a guy who had just tied up three dogs to a post outside Starbucks, and one of them looked like he had been abused. I went over and sat down with that dog, and he and Peanut both climbed into my lap. When the guy returned, he told me that the dog had been in and out of foster care because he didn't get along with other dogs and was probably going to be euthanized. I looked down at my lap at the two dogs curled up together and couldn't bear the idea of letting him die. I took him home that day and named him Turkey.

Turkey was the opposite of Peanut. He was rambunctious, he loved his toys and treats, he liked to play fetch and he let everybody know he was king of the house. Meanwhile, Peanut took on a mothering role. Every night after dinner she would lick Turkey's face. He would lie down in their bed and she would lie next to him, like two peas in a pod. We were the perfect trio.

In 2013, the three of us moved to Chicago. I had been living in San Francisco in a rent-controlled apartment for twelve years when the landlord sold the building. No longer able to afford the city's rising rents, I thought, *If I'm ever going to make a change in my life, now's the time.* I had money saved to change careers and go back to school. But since I wouldn't be working, I needed an affordable city with good community services for HIV, and Chicago offered that.

That winter was the polar vortex. I wasn't working or in school yet, and the isolation of being trapped in my house because it was forty degrees below zero outside pushed me into depression. Those months were among the darkest of my life, and I was kicking myself, thinking I'd made the wrong choice. But the option to stay in bed and forget about the world doesn't exist when you have a dog—let alone two dogs. Peanut and Turkey pushed me to get up and get on with our routine, which was a big help for my mental health. Turkey made me feel lighter, because he was always trying to play, and Peanut showered me with affection. With the two of them in my lap, I felt some of the happiest moments in my life.

I lost Turkey to heart disease in October. Having to make the decision to end Turkey's life was the hardest thing I've ever had to do. In our time together, Turkey brought me so much joy and laughter. Looking back on that, I can't help but think of the serendipity of it all: Fifteen years ago, I had been a guy who didn't want to take care of anyone but himself when I took a chance on Peanut. If it weren't for Peanut, I wouldn't have been out on that walk Thanksgiving Day. If I hadn't gone on that walk, I wouldn't have stopped by Starbucks, and I wouldn't have met Turkey. The way Turkey immediately took to Peanut and seeing them cuddled up together were what told me I needed to rescue him too.

I've been through some pretty tough times over the years. Without biological family to support me, those dogs were my motivation to go on. Adopting Peanut was the turning point in my life. She taught me the value in extending love and compassion to others, and in doing so, I found a family and fulfillment that I couldn't have imagined if I had never taken the chance.

I Carry Him in My Heart

HOOT & SPLOOT

ploot and I had a spiritual connection from the very beginning. I'd been wanting a dog for some time, and one day when I was home for spring break, I saw a photo from the local shelter of this dog with a funny little Mohawk that looked kind of like the Lorax. I knew I had to meet him.

The night before I went to the shelter, I dreamt that I couldn't take him home because he hadn't been neutered. The next day, when I went to meet him, I was halfway through the paperwork when a vet tech told me I might not be able to take Sploot home because he hadn't been neutered yet—it was uncanny and the first of many experiences when I've felt Sploot and I shared a spiritual kinship. Fortunately, there was a mix-up, and I did end up taking him home that day.

Three months later, I was diagnosed with HIV, and he once again proved to be in my life for a reason.

My partner of seven years and I had a mutual friend visit us one weekend in the spring. He wasn't HIV positive at the time, but at some point, that changed. When he was diagnosed a few months later, he called us and recommended a mobile tester who came to our apartment and tested my partner and me in our living room. Sploot was there, sitting on my lap the whole time. When the results came back, I tested positive and my partner didn't. I was crushed, and I couldn't help but feel jealous. I was trapped in what had become a toxic relationship, and I believed that no one else would love me or want to be with me now that I was HIV positive. I was completely broken.

For years, I kept my status to myself and my partner. I convinced myself that if I tried harder and compromised more, I could fix our failing relationship. Of course, I now know that never works.

After my diagnosis I lost all sense of myself. I had so much shame. I wasn't really eating and had developed a serious drinking problem. The HIV medication I was prescribed in Oklahoma had nasty side effects, including recurring nightmares and severe weight loss. I had no energy, chronic hip pain and neuropathy in my feet. When I asked to switch to a different pill, the doctor told me I'd have side effects no matter what and convinced me to stick with it. My health made it difficult to take Sploot out for walks as often as he needed, and when he had accidents inside, I felt awful for not taking care of him the way he deserved. But the reality was that I simply didn't know how to take care of myself.

Amid that darkness, I pushed everyone away except for Sploot. He understood that I was in a lot of pain, and he knew what I needed when I needed it. Sploot was never going to give up on me, and that gave me a reason to get out of bed. He gave my life structure and stability, and he never ceased to make me laugh—just by doing the smallest things, like how he'd lie down and kick his legs out like little drumsticks. A friend had told me that Corgi owners call that "splooting," so that's how he got his name.

When we moved to Madison, Wisconsin, my new doctor immediately changed my medication. As soon as I switched, I started to get my energy back and I was no longer battling chronic pain. My appetite improved a bit, so I started to put on some healthy weight and was feeling more like myself again. We were living with my ex on his family's old farm, so Sploot got free rein of twenty-six acres of open land. He was pure bliss out there, and I'm happy to have been able to give him that experience.

As I became stronger physically, I also became stronger mentally and emotionally. Eventually I mustered the courage to step out on my own—and that was in no small part thanks to Sploot's love and support.

Once we were free, I planned to buy an old Subaru and hit the road—just the two of us—but Sploot became sick and went blind suddenly. I looked for work and found us a more permanent living situation to start our new life together in Chicago. I'd had him with me in Chicago for a month when he suddenly developed a herniated disk. I rushed him to the emergency room and painfully came to the impossible decision to let him go. Making that call was one of the hardest things I've ever had to do, but Sploot had been so good to me through my pain, I owed it to him to give him a peaceful and pain-free death.

I've been through a lot of grief throughout my life, but losing Sploot was another level—even my HIV diagnosis pales in comparison. The first few weeks after his death felt chaotic. For my entire life up to that point, I'd had to take care of other people. As a kid, I took care of my mom, who is disabled. Then I graduated to taking care of my ex-partner, who suffered myriad health problems, and finally I had Sploot—my first real companion and the first time I experienced unconditional love. Without him I had no one left to care for but myself. I felt the depths of true loneliness, and it was terrifying.

In the months since, I've come to see that this loss has been a necessary lesson for me. Dogs teach us a lot about our character, and caring for Sploot taught me radical empathy. He not only taught me how to be there for others, but how to walk away and set healthy boundaries. After a lifetime of putting the needs of others first, I needed to finally make myself a priority.

When Dogs Heal

After Sploot died, I decided to quit smoking and my anxiety is much easier to manage. I have learned to lean into my pain and seek out opportunities to heal rather than hide from it. I am probably the healthiest that I have ever been, because I am finally being true to myself and comfortable in my skin. Sploot's love was a driving force behind all of that.

Participating in *When Dogs Heal* felt like an important opportunity in my journey to help others who are battling the shame that comes from an HIV diagnosis, addiction or mental illness. When I think about everything that Sploot did for me—from helping me address and work through toxic patterns to changing the way I see the world—he has created lasting goodness in my life. He helped me love and accept myself, and I want to do that for others.

Sploot saw me through the most traumatic years of my adult life and helped me emerge on the other side as a better person. Though I wish I could see him, I still think about him every day and I carry his love and the lessons he taught me in my heart wherever I go.

When I Need Them the Most

BRANDON, ECHO, NIKE & AJAX

Back in August of 2012, I found out the guy I'd been with for a year and a half had been cheating on me. Pretty cool, huh?

He was a consultant and traveled for work Monday through Friday. I grew suspicious when he started missing our nightly phone calls, until one weekend a text preview from a name I didn't recognize popped up on his phone that said: "I love you so much. You should move to Denver with me." He had no choice but to come clean. I was devastated.

In the wake of that betrayal, it was my Labrador, Echo, who kept me sane. He was my best buddy and more. The way someone might come home from work to their partner and say, "Honey, I'm home," I would do that with Echo.

After my ex and I broke up, I was single and dating around. By Christmas that year, I had the worst flu in the world that would not go away, and I looked like a ghost. That's when I first got a hunch that I'd been exposed to the virus.

I hadn't always been irresponsible. I used to get tested religiously every three or four months, but after that breakup I didn't get tested again until February 2013—one of the longest periods since I'd become sexually active. I was going through a dark time and letting my depression play out with uncharacteristically risky behaviors. I felt like, *who cares?*

In February, I finally dragged myself to a local health clinic to get tested. While waiting for results, the doctor suggested that I might be a good candidate for a new anti-HIV medication that could keep HIV-negative people from becoming infected— it was the first I'd heard of what we now know as PrEP. When the doctor came back holding the test in a gloved hand, I knew it was too late. He said, "These two lines mean we need to have a different conversation than we were just having." I started to cry.

That night, I went to my friend's house and drank two bottles of wine. The next day, I went back to the doctor, where they took what felt like fifty thousand tubes of blood, and I began treatment. The first medication I started was one pill a day, and the gastrointestinal side effects were awful. I thought, *If this is the rest of my life, fuck this.* It played into the narrative that my life was over, that this was what HIV would be like. There was a steep learning curve—I didn't know anything about viral loads or T cells or prognosis. Facing what I perceived to be a major health crisis, I thought I needed to get my will in order and announce beneficiaries, so I decided to disclose my status to my mother and brother.

It was not easy. I'd had a bad experience when I came out to my dad at nineteen. He told me I was gross and disgusting and he didn't want to speak with me. We didn't talk for a year. With HIV there was the same fear that my parents wouldn't accept me, because I was different again. My dad's words were in the back of my head when I told my mom. Fortunately, she and my brother were supportive. Still, I had trouble leaning on them because I was embarrassed and ashamed of myself. I've never been able to reopen that wound with my father, so he doesn't know about my HIV diagnosis to this day.

That's when I realized how important Echo was. I was living by myself, and when I'd come home from the doctor's office or from work, Echo would be there. I would talk to him about what I was going through, tell him when I felt sad, stressed or scared. To Echo, it didn't matter if I felt bad or good, if I was positive or not. If anything, me being sick made him more like Velcro—he attached himself to me at the first sign I was down. Coming home to his wagging tail and kisses when I didn't feel like I deserved a wagging tail and kisses, or even to be touched, was a reminder that I wasn't unlovable or dangerous.

After I tested positive, Echo was my motivation to get and stay healthy, take my meds and go to doctors' appointments. When you have a dog in the city—especially a larger breed—you don't have a choice but to get up off your rear end to take him on walks. If I hadn't had him to push me, I probably would have locked myself in my house for days.

My doctors recommended that I tie my HIV medication to some aspect of my day so it would become routine, so I coupled it with Echo's evening meal and walk. I knew he wouldn't let me forget to feed him, so his reminder would initiate the process: food, walk, medication. Since I started treatment, I've never missed a dose. Echo played a major role in that.

I had to put Echo down in December 2015, two years after my diagnosis. He had a long life, but it was still devastating. I was feeling better and healthy by that point, but that last gift he gave to me was important—he kept me from spiraling. Losing him was, in some ways, worse than learning I had HIV, and I told myself I could never get a dog again. I tried to replace what Echo had been providing by traveling more and telling myself life would be easier. In reality, it was awful. It screwed up my schedule, I'd come home at night to my empty apartment and think, *This is boring and lame.* I didn't realize how therapeutic it had been to have him there as a constant source of love and support. I only lasted a month before I put a deposit down on Nike.

For the first six months, having a puppy again and potty training in a high-rise apartment was a challenge, but it was good for me. Even when he didn't mean to, Nike was getting me off the couch and out socializing with other humans. Nike picked up the baton where Echo left off. However, it soon became clear that I might not be the only one who needed help. Nike had bad separation anxiety and would cry all day while I was at work. A friend of mine had just gotten a second dog and said it revolutionized her older dog's life. That's how I got Ajax in 2016, and now our pack of three is complete.

If I thought one Lab was a lot of exercise and outdoor time, it's even more with two. Every time we go out, it's an adventure. I live in Uptown, because it's close to Puptown, one of the best dog parks in Chicago. We are within walking distance of Montrose dog beach on Lake Michigan, where we play fetch for hours in the warm months. I've made friends at the park and beach too.

Many things I didn't even realize Echo was providing, Nike and Ajax provide too. Whenever my stomach was cramping from my HIV meds, or if I was feeling sad, I would sit on the floor of my shower and let the hot water pour over me for hours. Labradors are water dogs, so Echo developed this habit of sticking his nose around the corner of the shower curtain to remind me when it was time to eat and start our evening routine. Nike and Ajax started to do the same thing—like, *hey, there's water in there—we're coming in!* Some days it was easy to let depression take control. To see a little black nose poke into the shower was enough to make me laugh.

I'm pretty open about my status with people now, though I am not sure I'll ever tell my dad. We're on much better terms than we were, but I feel the potential negatives still outweigh the positives. I hope this book might be an opportunity to change his view of HIV-positive people.

Society has built in some component of shame or stigma that occasionally nags at me. I myself had never met an HIV-positive person before I moved to Chicago; it was a scary thing that I didn't understand. When I first started dating here, I don't know that I would have slept with someone positive even with a condom. That didn't change until I was forced to face my own diagnosis. I was part of the stigma.

Echo—and now Nike and Ajax—have played a critical role in my self-acceptance and the mental transition from being negative to positive. They have had a profound influence on my happiness. Today, I keep Echo's ashes in a wooden urn above my bed, where he continues to keep watch over me as he did in those early days when I needed him most.

A Space in the World

LISA & MIMI

Early in life, I had to fight to be myself and have my own space in the world. When I was fourteen, my mother caught me dressing up as a girl and threw me out of the house. I lived on the streets until a friend's mother allowed me to stay with them. My father was working in Miami at the time. When he came home a month later and found out what had happened, he got me a room at a boardinghouse for twenty-five dollars a week; he wanted me to have a place where I could be me but also be safe.

This was the early 1970s; it was illegal to be transgender in Puerto Rico. Even though I had to be careful dressing up in public, I wasn't going to change who I was. Most fathers in our community wouldn't have tolerated a gay son—especially their firstborn—but whenever my mother would hit me for my effeminate behavior, mine intervened because he saw that I was smart and worked hard.

A few months after I moved to the boardinghouse, I heard about an opportunity to perform at El Cotorrito (the Little Parrot), a female impersonator club in San Juan. Drag performances were also illegal then, but the club owner had a license because he did free graphic design work for the party in power. I'd been dancing for years in jazz, ballet and flamenco and knew I could be a great performer, but because I was a minor, my father had to sign a letter granting me permission to work. All I wanted was to make my own money and take care of myself. The moment I entered that club I became Ginger Valdez. I wasn't putting on a dress and makeup just for fun anymore—I was a professional.

In November 1976 our show traveled to New York, and while I was there, I fell in love. I was eighteen and he was forty-one. He had a job and an apartment. He was very responsible and very handsome. When the two-month show was up, he asked me to move in with him. I thought, *What have I got to lose?* And I stayed for almost ten years.

That man was the love of my life. When we broke up, I was devastated—I felt abandoned, reckless and alone. I started smoking crack and escorting. Though I never let either take over my life, I knew what I was doing was not right. I had a lot of bad relationships, and somewhere along the way I contracted HIV.

When I tested positive, I wasn't in shock. It was the eighties and HIV was everywhere, but I really didn't expect it to happen to me. It's not that I wasn't afraid, but I don't anticipate the worst. I thought, *If I have to live with this virus, then I will. If at some point that means I'll endure pain or disadvantage, I will face it.* One foot in front of the other—that's how I managed to survive as a kid living on my own. Fortunately, my CD4 T-cell count was high, so I educated myself and made sure I ate well, exercised, kept up with my vitamins and took care of myself.

When I was thirty-three, I came to Chicago to emcee two drag pageants at the Baton Show Lounge. I was ready for a different pace. In New York, everything happened so fast—good and bad. I saw friends get killed, overdose or die of AIDS. I did things that I knew were hurting me, and I was tired of all that. I decided that I had more important things to do—not just for me but for others.

I decided to stay in Chicago for good and joined an organization called Minority Outreach Intervention Program (MOIP). The trans population is the most underserved and mistreated part of the LGBTQ community, and transgender African Americans and Latinas in particular were dropping like flies. I knew the experience firsthand. If I was sick and went to the hospital, I'd be treated poorly because of the way I looked and for my sexual orientation. It was degrading and it hurt. Through MOIP, Transgender Women Involved in Strategies for Transformation (TWIST), and several other organizations over the last two decades, I've been able to give HIV-positive transwomen a better quality of life—from managing their health and relationships to medication and support networks.

When it came to my personal support network, I had Mimi.

When I first got Mimi, I was still grieving the loss of my previous dog, Yunya, who—after lifting me out of the loneliest years of my life—died unexpectedly. The pain was so great that the day after she passed, I landed in the hospital's intensive care unit because my right lung, compromised by chronic obstructive pulmonary disease, a respiratory inflammation, nearly collapsed from how hard I'd been crying.

Six months later, when I was still in a bad place, Mimi came into my life. She gave me the spark that I needed. When Mimi sees me crying, she starts whining to get me to stop. If I am depressed, I know I cannot risk a situation that may damage my well-being or mental stability, because I need to take care of her.

To give you a better idea of how much I love my dogs: I used to have a queen-size bed. After Mimi gave birth this year, I bought an expensive mahogany king-size bed. I sleep on one edge and Mimi and her puppies take the rest of the bed, but I don't care because I got it for them. I even had a staircase built so they could come up and down as they please.

They have their sweaters for fall and their coats for winter, because I need to make sure they're comfortable. If it's getting late at work, I tell my supervisor, "No, I have to go to my dogs." I get so much joy just knowing that I can provide for them; getting to feed and spend time with them each night is the icing on the cake.

When I come through the door, Mimi starts barking and jumping all over me, which makes me feel loved and wanted. That reaction is so important to my mental health. We play and she kisses me, and I tell her how much I missed her and how much I love her.

When it's time to sleep, I say, "Mimi, let's go nighty night," and she and her pups follow me into bed. On Sundays, I take them to one of three big parks nearby. I bring a bottle of water and a dish for them, and if there aren't other dogs around, I let them off the leash and watch them run.

Those animals are everything to me. It has been six years since I've been in a romantic relationship—young people look for young people, and old people look for young people too. But dogs don't care whether you're young or old. They just want you to give them love and kindness, so they can give that right back to you.

I don't have any blood relatives in or near Chicago—my son who lives with me is not by blood (though he's been in my life for a long time). In Puerto Rico, I was raised in one of the biggest caserios, or housing projects, in San Juan. My neighbors and I saw one another grow up—we went to one another's birthdays and funerals. It was like being a part of a huge, extended family. Having Mimi and her puppies around me provides that same feeling. There's a sense of community and home.

My babies are free to do whatever they want in my home. I don't put them in cages or close doors, they can go up and downstairs as they wish, they can jump on the sofa for all I care, and nobody can say anything! This is my space, and in it Mimi is queen.

When Dogs Save

RJ & STOLI

was diagnosed with AIDS after having a stroke. I don't know who found me first. I was knocked out cold, lying on my bed. I was only twenty-nine years old. Based on my medical history, the doctors figured that I had probably been living with AIDS for the past ten years, which made sense. Ten years earlier my only boyfriend had been cheating on me. I was immediately rushed to the emergency room, and during the initial treatment, my body rejected everything the doctors gave me. I don't remember a lot, but I know my family and my best friend were there. He said he was praying to God that I wouldn't die.

Fortunately, their prayers worked. I was eventually released from the hospital, but I did not take HIV medication for years after that because I was so ashamed. The first doctor I saw made me feel disgusting, like I was less than a person because of my status. I just wanted to block it all out. Medications were a reminder of being HIV positive. And back then, any day that I was not reminded about my HIV status was a good day. When I got stronger, I returned to work and tried to get back into a routine and conduct my life as normal, but I struggled. I became reclusive. I shut out my friends and family for years as I tried to ignore the reality of my health situation.

In 2007, I got my own apartment using a medical and housing assistance program for people with disabilities. It should have been exciting, but I ended up sitting in the house by myself 24/7 and I grew even more isolated and lonely. One day, my best friend came over with a dog that I assumed was his. But instead, he told me he'd gotten the dog for me. "Your stubborn ass needs this dog to love you," he said. "You love him back or your ass is going to die."

I was resistant. Truth is, I was scared. I'd become so used to being alone that I didn't want to be bothered with a dog, and I was afraid I couldn't care for him. The stroke left me wheelchair-bound, and I couldn't imagine walking him or taking care of him. I tried to explain that to my friend. In fact, we fought about it. In the end, my friend just looked at me and said, "You're smart, you're resourceful." Then he walked out of my apartment, leaving me with a puppy. A puppy, of all things. When I looked down into Stoli's eyes, it happened instantly: I fell in love.

It turned out that having Stoli was the opposite of the prison I had allowed my life with HIV to become. Living with Stoli was freeing. I had gotten so used to being alone and inside that I'd forgotten the warmth of the sun and the beauty of the birds chirping outside. It gave me hope to see that dog so happy, even as I just rode around in my wheelchair. I hadn't felt happiness like that in quite some time. I had forgotten how good it could feel.

The more time we spent outside together, the more I tried to use my legs again. The doctors thought that at best, I'd be able to learn how to walk with a walker. But after time—thanks to Stoli's support—I began walking almost as if nothing had ever happened to me. Stoli taught me how to walk again. He taught me not to hide from the world anymore.

A few years later, with Stoli by my side, I fell in love. But once again, it ultimately did not work and my heart was broken. At that point, all I wanted to do was leave Miami. I needed a fresh start. I decided to move to Atlanta to build a better life for Stoli and me. Because I didn't have a job, I stayed with my brother. I hoped to get housing through an HIV assistance program, but no one would take me because I had a dog. Even though I knew my brother loved me, I felt like a burden living there and began feeling worse and worthless. One day—after working for two weeks straight—I was tired and frustrated. Still hurting from having my heart broken, I decided I couldn't do it anymore. Everything in my life just felt so hard. I needed it all to end, so I decided I was going to kill myself.

I had two bottles of extra-strength Tylenol, some sleeping pills and Benadryl—I was going for the gusto. I wanted it to be done. I sat on my bed staring at the bottles on my dresser from across the room, contemplating whether I wanted to do this. I was hopeless. It was the darkest moment of my life. When I decided to take the pills, I got up and before I could reach the bottles, Stoli jumped on the bed. He looked so happy as always. He needed me, and I believe in that moment he was telling me not to do what I had planned. He suddenly wanted to go out. His needs became more important than mine. It was like a jolt went through my body. Immediately, that changed my thoughts.

When I took him outside, I heard the birds singing again as I had during our first walks. I thought to myself, *I can fight for one more day.* When we got back inside, I looked at those bottles and I flushed the pills down the toilet. I have been fighting every day since. After that day, I vowed to never give up and never allow myself to get that low again.

Sometimes I joke with people that I am a country song waiting to be written. The only thing I own on this earth is my dog and my truck, but for the first time in my life, that's more than enough for me to feel complete. I have faith and I am working again. I see each step, even the tiny ones, as progress. While they may not be big steps, I trust that they will lead to a better tomorrow for Stoli and me. My past will not define my future. And thanks to the love of family, friends and of course Stoli, I am whole again.

Appreciate What You Have

BARRY & LOLA

didn't want to take an HIV test at first. It was 1995, I had just checked into rehab for alcohol and drug abuse, and I already felt like life was an uphill battle. I had been drinking since high school, and in college I crossed that invisible line into addiction, which continued when I moved to New York City after graduation. I didn't think I could break that long-ingrained habit and handle a death sentence on top of it.

At the time, other than the very harsh AZT, there were no real options for treatment. As a volunteer for Gay Men's Health Crisis in New York, I spent hours at a time helping one young person after the next draft wills, elect powers of attorney, and find bereavement groups. I watched my best friend—a vibrant, young, smart guy—wither away from AIDS. It scared the shit out of me.

We had been young, living in New York City and doing everything we'd always wanted to do. Nobody knew much about HIV. One day people would say it was caused by poppers, the next by unprotected sex. People said if you drank kombucha, you'd be fine. I had a friend who became convinced to mix a tablespoon of bleach with a cup of water and drink it a couple of times a day. So much misinformation was floating around, and nobody knew what to believe. Plus, there was so little action being taken by the government to prevent it. As information did emerge, there was a general sense that if you were gay, you were going to get AIDS. It became easier to simply avoid thinking about it, because what could you do?

So, while my HIV diagnosis was certainly devastating, I sort of expected it. I just didn't think I could overcome addiction while at the same time waiting to die. In hindsight, going to rehab turned out to be the best thing that could have happened to me. Had I not already been in the process of getting sober when I tested positive, it's likely that when I heard the news I would have gone on a bender. Drugs and alcohol would have killed me first.

While getting sober, I learned to accept the things I could not change. I couldn't change the fact that I had HIV. All I could do was figure out how to move forward and live the best and healthiest life I could for as long as I could. After rehab, I moved into a sober living house with a group of fifteen friends with whom I'd gone to meetings and endured the journey of recovery. After six to eight months, they all started relapsing. I began to think it was inevitable, part of the process even, and that I would relapse too. Fortunately, I spoke to a sober mentor who helped me see that I didn't have to fall into that pattern, and I'm proud to say that in twenty-four years, I never have.

Once I became sober, I knew I needed something to love and hang on to. Around that time in Los Angeles it was the hot thing for people to adopt miniature potbelly pigs, so I tried that first. I loved that pig and took him for walks, but over time he got bigger and bigger until he weighed 150 pounds. It was clear that he wasn't the miniature breed I'd been sold, and I had to give him to a farm. Shortly thereafter, I met my life partner, John, and together we adopted a bulldog named Brutus. In that moment, the die was cast. We both fell in love with being dog owners, and we've had dogs ever since.

From the very beginning, Brutus changed my life. At six months old, he became my constant companion. He slept in bed with us every night and went to work with me every day at a private girls' school, where the students loved him so much they put him in the yearbook. John was working long hours, so I was usually on my own to feed and walk him. Caring for Brutus taught me a sense of responsibility I had been sorely lacking when I was in the throes of addiction.

Years later, we got talked into adopting our second dog, Chester, when a friend of ours saw him running on the freeway in the freezing rain. Chester was emaciated and showed obvious signs of abuse. When we first met him, he was cowering in the corner. He was afraid of everybody, but for whatever reason he liked me and let me play with him. I instantly fell in love, and we cherished our years with Chester until he passed. We recently lost our third dog, Jasper, just before I had to have a hip replacement. For a few months our house was quiet and I missed having dogs like crazy. I kept telling John that I wanted another. I know some people need more time after losing a pet, but I've never seen adopting a new dog as replacing the old one—I see it as expanding our love, giving another animal in need an opportunity for a home.

John didn't think it was a good idea because I was still recovering from my procedure and could hardly get around. Ten days into bed rest, I decided I couldn't wait. I saw a couple puppies online I wanted to meet, and John—though he thought I was crazy—let me drag him to see them, despite me still being dependent on a walker. We came home with Lola, who made the remaining two months of my recovery infinitely better. It would have taken twice as long for my hip to heal, and it wouldn't have healed properly had I not been so committed to physical therapy, thanks to her. As soon as I could use a cane, I started taking Lola for walks. She was good about staying right next to me. She didn't pull or try to run away; she was patient. As Lola learned how to be a dog, so to speak, she helped me heal and get stronger.

Before I got sober, I thought only about my needs. Addiction makes you selfish, self-centered and self-seeking. Having dogs has challenged me to consider factors outside of my life and experience and meet them with compassion. For instance, Lola is afraid of thunder and lightning. No matter how much I try to comfort her, to tell her that it's okay and she's safe, whenever it storms she runs into the closet to hide. All I want in that moment is to understand how I can be there for her and to ease her suffering. At some point, I realized, what if I could afford other people that same compassion? Now, if I encounter someone who is acting out in a way that frustrates me, rather than become annoyed, I try to think, *Okay, maybe that person's being a jerk, but maybe they're going through something that I don't understand.*

Those shifts in my attitude and mindset helped me redefine who I was. Before I was a dog owner, I felt like I didn't know what I wanted out of life or who I was. All that mattered was being a big shot in the big city. The more I spent time with my dogs and my partner, the more I learned that what was really important was to love and care about someone.

I was diagnosed with Parkinson's disease about two years ago. Once again, I had to accept the things I could not change. The old me would have spent my days wondering, *Why me? Why is the world against me?* Through time and learning, I don't feel that way anymore. HIV really prepared me to take this in stride. My experience has taught me to tackle challenges in manageable bites, rather than letting it all explode and then hiding in my bed and weeping for a month. I learned early on from HIV that you don't miss doses of your medication, and the same goes for Parkinson's. I go to the gym three times a week and I box twice a week because it is really good for my disease. I focus on how I can move forward, I keep myself as healthy as possible and I continue to fight.

Having a dog has made me stronger, kinder and showed me what matters. Lola knows when I'm unhappy; she knows when I'm sick. She is never too busy or disinterested to spend time with me. All she wants is to make me feel loved. Anytime I hit a rough spell, I know that I can hold her and hug her and I will ultimately feel better, because a dog shows you how to appreciate what you have.

A Loving Home

SAANTI BONET & ADUTCHESS

will never forget the day I found out I was HIV positive. It was August 13, 2014, and I was twenty-four years old. I am very in tune with my body, so after a week of feeling fatigued and weak, with no sign of getting better, I knew something wasn't right.

I went to an open mic night in Chicago where they were doing free HIV testing, and I decided to go for it. After a few minutes, the clinician pulled me aside and told me that I had tested positive—I realized that I had been feeling sick all week because I was seroconverting. I was baffled. My first thought was, *Me?! How dare you!* I have always been very smart and responsible about my health—I worked as a certified nursing assistant. I felt like a disgrace and that I should have known better.

A few months earlier, I had gotten out of what I thought was a committed relationship with a man who I loved very deeply. I believed our relationship was solid, so I let my guard down and trusted him enough to have unprotected sex. To learn he had not just been sleeping around but that he'd been careless and irresponsible about it, compromising my health while I was home trying to be Mrs. Right, made me angry. But more than that, I was hurt.

After I tested positive, I became suicidal. I wasn't in a great place as it was: I had recently been the target of discrimination at work and lost my job because of it. Unable to afford my rent, I was facing homelessness. To now have to deal with an HIV diagnosis on top of it, I thought, *Forget it, it's too hard.*

Especially in the Black community, there is a lot of hostility around HIV. Where I went to high school on the West Side of Chicago, reputation is everything. No one wants to be different. Even though HIV is a real threat to our community, people are more concerned with keeping up with the Joneses (whether it's getting designer clothes or an Escalade truck) than going to the doctor or talking about safe sex.

In my case, my foster mother was sixty-four when I was in high school—I actually call her my grandmother—so while she made sure I had what I needed in terms of food and clothing, sex and those types of things just weren't discussed. And with HIV in particular, the conversation was never harm-reductive or constructive; it was nasty, negative and reactive. There was this sense in our neighborhood that if you're positive, you'd better not tell anyone because people will talk badly about you and you will be publicly shamed. That, combined with my own disappointment, was more than I could handle.

One night, I drank a bunch of alcohol and hoped I wouldn't wake up. When I regained consciousness, my phone was ringing. It was my nephew asking whether I was still coming over to see him that weekend. When I heard his voice, I realized that I had reasons to live.

As a product of the foster care system since birth, love has not always been a given in my life. I lived in twenty-one foster homes before I was fifteen, so I spent most of my life trying to find stability with and in other people. Humans need each other. Growing up in situations where I didn't feel wanted, I would do anything to be with someone who would love me back.

That insecurity was enforced when I moved in with my grandmother after learning of my diagnosis. Though she had always said she loved me, she was uneducated about HIV and ostracized me because of my status. She labeled a specific chair, paper cups and paper plates with my name on them, and after I used them she would throw them away. I thought she would be my ultimate support system, so her behavior was really hurtful. Eventually I couldn't take it anymore and threatened to leave. She said that if I left, then I shouldn't come back—so I didn't. I spent more than four years couch surfing, sleeping on trains and staying with a client who I met while working as an escort to get back on my feet. When I finally did get back on my feet, I told myself, if I want to love and be loved unconditionally, then I should get a dog. A dog will be there no matter what—that's who they are, what they do, what they stand for. Adutchess has been exactly that.

New to having a home and job again, I had to adjust my mindset. Adutchess brought the sense of order and stability to my life that I needed. Having her to come home to every day is the reason I have been able to adhere to my medication. She wakes me up every day at 7:30 a.m., I take my medication and then I shower. Before I leave, I set out water and food bowls for her and replace the puppy pads. If there's a day I don't want to get up, when I feel I can't face my life, it's like she can feel my pain. On one of those days, when my stomach was hurting, she curled up next to me in bed and licked my stomach. That comfort alone was enough to get me up and out, and then it was easier to move on with my day.

She has given me a place to feel secure and at home. I want to make sure she's safe, so I am more selective about who I let into our lives and space. She can sniff out if someone is trustworthy, and if she doesn't like someone, then I won't. She keeps me focused and provides clarity. Every time I look into her beautiful brown eyes, I am inspired again to go forward and reminded that I want to live. She didn't choose to be with me—I chose her—and so I owe her a good and stable life. I love to spoil her—I give her everything a dog could dream of. She has almost more clothes than me, and I'm a shopaholic!

Though I have never again gotten as low as I did that night after my diagnosis, there's still an underlying fear around my status. This diagnosis is real—I have to deal

When Dogs Heal

with it every day, and staying on top of it is not something to be played with or taken lightly. Adutchess has taught me that the way I treat her—my baby—is how I need to treat my HIV. If you love your baby, you take care of that baby, you make sure she is okay. It is the same with HIV.

The biggest change in my life since adopting Adutchess is that I'm happier. She makes it okay to find joy. She oozes love—she can't even help it—and has provided me with a sense of purpose not only as a woman but as a human. Every person needs that.

A Search for Intimacy

BRENT, SALLY & MONTY

n some ways, my first addiction was a desperate search for intimacy.

My family was never close. My dad was a workaholic and rarely around, and even when he was, no one in our household ever talked about their feelings or said, "I love you." When I first left for school, I thought that was normal, but it became evident that I'd never really learned how to communicate my feelings and needs or be vulnerable with others—all of which prevented me from developing intimate relationships.

Deeper into my twenties, those needs began to express themselves in dangerous ways. I started experimenting with drugs, and I used them as a vehicle for seeking that intimacy through unprotected sex. To put it differently, my second addiction, meth, added a significant level of risk to my first addiction, intimacy.

When I was twenty-six, I found a lump in one of my armpits, which the doctor told me was one of two things: lymphoma or HIV. Spoiler: it wasn't lymphoma.

Coming of age during the worst years of the AIDS epidemic in a conservative suburban town in Oklahoma, I'd long held a morose, self-defeating view of HIV and AIDS. HIV was a death sentence and "God's punishment to gay people." That paranoia manifested in the fifty-plus HIV tests I'd already taken by that time and the two weeks I spent imagining my own horrible death while I waited for the results each time.

Oddly enough, when I took the test that finally gave me the positive diagnosis I'd long feared, I wasn't terribly anxious. That was because it was 1999 and treatment options were much better than they'd been even a few years earlier, and because by that point I was well into what would become a twenty-year, tumultuous relationship with meth that has always felt far worse than HIV.

My lowest point came in 2014 after I had moved to New York and was pursuing a lifelong dream of being a speech and debate coach at an elite prep school. The job was extremely demanding, requiring that we travel and compete every weekend, and it took a toll on me. One evening, a neighbor called the cops on me. While high on meth, I also suffered from a manic episode later associated with bipolar I disorder. I was found wandering my neighborhood, confused and disoriented, having an acutely psychotic episode. The police charged me with burglary even though I hadn't stolen anything. They ended up dropping the charges, but an article ran in the newspaper and the story haunts me to this day.

I went to rehab but relapsed later that year, and for years thereafter, delusions and paranoia came along whenever I used. After one incident—in which I fell off a fire escape and broke my elbow and foot and my kidneys started failing—my best friend came to the hospital and said he couldn't be my friend anymore, because he couldn't continue to watch me hurt myself. I understand it now, but at the time it was hard to stomach because I was already down.

Eventually I found a cocktail of four psych medications that miraculously seemed to work. When I started to show signs of improvement, I consulted with my medical team and they agreed it would be a great idea for me to adopt a dog to help with my health-care regimen.

Almost immediately, Sally gave me the accountability I needed. From the moment I first held her, something in me changed. I was overcome with emotion and a parental instinct. I understood that she was vulnerable and was depending on me to protect her. From that moment on, my world no longer revolved around me, my problems, my trauma.

As I succeeded in ensuring Sally's health, happiness and training, my self-worth improved. Like many addicts, when I was using I felt like I was a piece of shit, not worthy of respect. I couldn't take care of myself, much less another living thing. Watching Sally thrive—and hearing others praise her good behavior—made me realize that I was capable and reliable.

In 2018, my dad died unexpectedly and I had to find homes for his dogs. I was more or less estranged from my dad at that point, and it was evident that he hadn't been taking very good care of his dogs as his own health had started to decline. One dog in particular, Monty, was in bad shape. Not only was he old and less desirable to adopt, but his hair was patchy and matted, he was extremely overweight and he had heartworms. So I ended up taking him in. Neglected and eager for affection, maybe I saw a piece of myself in him. Maybe we both were worthy of redemption.

Since I adopted him, Monty's health has done a complete one-eighty. That has been a major accomplishment for me. There was a long period in which I couldn't take care of myself. When I was using, I never took my HIV medication. I couldn't be counted on to go to the bathroom or to drink water when I was using, much less take care of a dog. Proving I can take care of my dogs and myself has really helped boost my self-esteem, which was hurting after my diagnosis and when I lost myself in drugs and reckless behavior. I had a lot of guilt and shame, as most addicts do. I felt like I was a terrible person, and with the things drugs did to me physically, I felt like I was ugly, unattractive and unreliable—everything that makes a person good, I felt like I was the opposite.

Now, with Sally and Monty, I am the head of a household. I put systems in place so we can work together to keep things running and stay healthy—when the dogs get fed, when I feed myself, where the dog food is, when I take my pills, where my pills are kept. I am the necessary force to make sure all of that happens.

Over years of me not showing up for others and relapsing, I'd completely decimated my support system and I'm still struggling to rebuild that. But I've been sober for three years now, and I have learned to communicate what I need, how I feel and how to share love. I couldn't have done it without these two beautiful creatures, and I am proud of the job I have done in raising them. My devotion to caring for Monty and raising Sally in some ways feels like I am making up for the relationship my father and I never had.

In raising Sally and giving Monty a second chance at life, I am building the loving household I craved all those years ago.

Timing Is Everything

JASON & GIGI

was diagnosed with HIV on February 14, 2013—the Valentine's Day gift that keeps on giving. At the same time, my now ex-husband decided that our relationship was over. Part of the reason he left is he discovered I was using crystal meth.

My ex traveled a lot for work. As our communication started slipping, I stopped finding comfort in his company and started finding it in the company of others. We were open in our relationship, but eventually, every time he would leave there would be something or someone to fill that void. When he discovered I was using, I was honest about what was going on. Somewhere in the back of my mind I think I wanted to be caught—maybe some part of me was saving myself.

We agreed to separate, but first we both got tested. He came back negative and I came back positive. I don't know where I'd be right now if he'd tested positive. I went to rehab twice that year, and that thought is what took me back the second time. It was a dark time of my own doing. I felt a lot of shame and blamed myself for a lot of things. On some level I felt I deserved my diagnosis.

My doctor told me I should hold off on medication until I was ready to get sober and take care of myself. I got sober that August and have stayed sober ever since. The first HIV medication I was on caused a lot of stomach issues. I switched before I returned to rehab the second time, and by March I felt better—just in time for Gigi to come into my life.

Timing is everything.

I was in Union Square with my roommate, who had a dog, and I was talking about getting a dog as well. Moments later, we walked into Best Buy and there was a guy in there with an adorable French bulldog. He gave me his breeder's info, and I quickly became the first person on his list. It felt like a higher-power moment.

When I found out I was getting Gigi, it freaked me out at first. I was worried about having someone to take care of—I'd never done well caring for myself on my own. But when I met her, it was love at first sight. I remember talking to my sponsor, and he told me I needed to learn the meaning of unconditional love. (Everything was based on conditions with my ex, towards the end especially.) Gigi did that for me.

That first year of sobriety was really tough. Shortly after I got her, I started making trips back to Chicago. My dad needed surgery to repair his failing pacemaker, and he stayed in the ICU for ten days. We just didn't know if he was going to survive.

Gigi came with me to the nursing home, and it surprised me how she instinctively knew what to do to help others. I remember seeing her put her front paws up on the wheel of a woman's wheelchair and look at her reassuringly, allowing the woman to pet her. My dad died about three months later, and Gigi came with me to the funeral. During that period, I watched how big of an impact she had on my mom's life, on the lives of other sick and grieving people and of course on me.

Taking Gigi to hospitals and nursing homes, and watching how her presence could lift people up, helped me realize that I could be of service to others and that has rebuilt my self-esteem again. Before her, I felt very alone and isolated. She got me out of the house and kept me moving through bouts of depression and anxiety. She brought people back into my life. I slowly got to know my neighbors and started to become part of a community again. This six-pound puppy tore at everyone's heartstrings—suddenly people who had stopped coming around wanted to spend time with us. Whether they wanted to spend it with Gigi or with me, it didn't matter. We were a package deal.

When I was first starting over after my diagnosis, I had almost nobody. I had a few friends, but most of them didn't want to speak to me. Gigi helped me see that as a catalyst for rebuilding. She helped me find opportunity for new ways to live.

She started coming with me to sober meetings. Having her there was like having a social lubricant. I can put on a great front, but I can be uncomfortable in social situations, and her presence puts me at ease. She helped me create boundaries. For most of my life, I was a people pleaser—I would do whatever I could to make other people happy, even if it didn't make me happy. Gigi gave me the confidence to interact with people in a more honest way—even if that's just telling someone that they are not petting her the right way.

Now if a visitor comes late at night, she barks. I don't want the neighbors to complain, so I don't have late-night companions anymore, and that helps prevent me from doing things that I know can be detrimental to my life. Gigi has given me the accountability and responsibility I needed. Her schedule has become my schedule. I take my pills before we go out, and I've started to feel stronger.

She's taught me that I can't always be in control (she's stubborn and tends to like things *her* way). That got me out of my head and helped me create a new idea of myself. I've learned to adjust my thinking. For my parents, success was based on material possessions and money. But since having her, I've learned that success is based on being happy.

I worked in advertising for twenty years, selling people things they didn't need. I had always talked about becoming a therapist or a social worker, but my dad told me not to because I wouldn't make any money. I am almost done with my first year of school to become a drug and alcohol counselor for others in the LGBT community struggling with addiction. This is my way of giving back, of using my own experiences to make things better. That's another thing I learned from her. Communication isn't always about what you say—it's about what you do.

Someone once told me that you always get the dog you deserve. As I was healing from all this, there were many moments when I thought that I had not only *done* things that were wrong, but that *I* was wrong somehow. But if that is true, then I didn't deserve her. If I was a bad person, I wouldn't have gotten a dog that makes people laugh just by walking down the street. I know that because I got Gigi, everything I've done in life hasn't been bad—there must be something in me that's redemption-worthy.

So, did Gigi save me? I don't know if she saved me, but she helped me find myself. She was the miracle that I needed.

Hearing Each Other

ADAM & LAILA

Having grown up in San Francisco, a progressive city where I'd participated in queer youth programming, I knew how to have "the talk" with partners. I knew to ask when they were last tested and about their results. And I did that consistently—I took all the right steps. Unfortunately, a guy I was seeing lied about his status. I found out when my routine six-month test came back positive. As the nurse held my hand, I started to cry. In that moment, I pictured myself at twenty-two years old in a hospital bed with tubes snaked through my nose and mouth. I said, "My family is going to be so disappointed in me."

I went home that night and cuddled with Laila, whom I'd adopted just three months before I received that diagnosis. For weeks after, I would wake up crying and stare at my reflection in disbelief, tears streaming down my face. I felt utterly defeated and hopeless. I was young—I didn't even have a primary care doctor yet! I told both my family and work within a few days of finding out because I didn't think I could process the diagnosis alone, but I'm not sure that it was the best thing to do. Even if people weren't saying anything to my face, I knew they were saying things behind my back, and my family quickly cut me out.

My family's reaction wasn't surprising. Both of my parents are immigrants. Dad is from China and Mom is from Burma. I'm their firstborn son and the oldest of ten children. Where they come from, being the firstborn son comes with a lot of privileges and responsibilities—being gay meant I wasn't living up to those responsibilities. When I came out at seventeen, my parents had told me I wasn't their son anymore, and that if they'd known I was going to be gay, then they wouldn't have had me. I tried to run away, but I didn't know where to go. When I came back a few hours later, my clothes were in a laundry basket on the sidewalk. I finished high school while staying with my best friend's family. My parents and I didn't speak for a year. Eventually my dad apologized, but our relationship had barely recovered when I had to come out again—this time as HIV positive.

When I sat them down, the first thing my mom said was, "I knew this was going to happen the day you told me you were gay." I was immediately disinvited to family dinners and parties. My brothers and sisters weren't allowed to come to my house anymore.

Once, I took my eight-year-old brother to the movies and as I was ordering food, he shouted, "I have to get my own water!" I knew that someone must have drilled that into him before they let him go out with me. These kinds of constant microaggressions hurt my feelings, but I didn't know how to stand up for myself. It was a lonely time. At one point, I actually started to think, *I am a diseased person and people shouldn't be around me.* Ignorance can be a strong beast.

Laila was an invaluable companion through all that. The stigma surrounding HIV didn't exist to Laila—she still sat next to me and slept next to me. My responsibility to take her out, to get some fresh air and get my brain to release endorphins is what helped keep depression at bay—especially as my body struggled to adjust to the medication. For weeks, I'd wake up in the night and stumble down the hallway or collapse onto the floor. When I was too sick to get up, Laila stood next to the bed and put her head on my chest (something she does to this day if I'm not feeling well). She'd wait there for nearly an hour at times to make sure I was okay.

It was scary. I was getting constant migraines, vivid dreams and was sensitive to sunlight, but I didn't know whether it was from the medication, the HIV or the stress. At the time, I was taking what I was told was the best pill on the market. Because people I knew were taking up to fifteen pills a day, I felt like I should just stick it out with this one. It would be years before I'd learn that these were common side effects of the medication and eventually switch to something my body could handle.

Going through the motions to care for Laila when all I wanted to do was stay in bed helped me build the momentum and stamina I needed to take care of myself. I started to ask questions like, *How do I tackle this diagnosis? Am I going to live, or am I going to die?* The demons were there, but I began to see a way out.

When I finally sat down and confronted my dad, I realized that he didn't have the words or the education to understand what HIV is today—how I couldn't give it to anyone through being bit by the same mosquito or by sharing a glass of water. After a difficult two-hour conversation with him, we went out to get dinner. At one point, I cut off a piece of his steak with my fork and when my dad moved the rest of the meat to my plate, I was disappointed. I thought, *After all that, he still doesn't get it.* "No," he said. "I'm giving it to you because you're clearly still hungry." Then he took the rest of the steak and shoved it into his mouth. It was funny. My dad's understanding of the world is different, but we were willing to hear each other.

Three months after I started medication, I decided to go to law school in Hawaii. It was a difficult decision because I wouldn't be able to take Laila, but I felt I needed to make a fresh start in a place where no one knew me. While I was away, Laila stayed with my roommate and my brother, and I came back every chance I could. Law school is where I became immersed in LGBT work—civil rights, antidiscrimination, HIV and policy.

That background led me to my current work speaking with high school students in the Bay Area about HIV and safer sex. It isn't easy to share my story and relive the memories of my diagnosis over and over again. It's raw and emotional, but doing it makes me feel like this horrible thing that happened was not for nothing.

Often the kids I speak to ask how I managed to lift myself up, to keep going when I was kicked out at seventeen. I tell them about the dream I had for my life as a kid: I'd go to college, get a job, get married, have children, a dog and a house—I simply never stopped reaching for those things. I wanted to prove wrong everyone who thought I couldn't turn my life around. I picked myself up, showed gratitude toward those who helped me along the way and continued working toward my goals. I got two part-time jobs my first year in college, applied for financial aid and kept putting one foot in front of the other.

Eleven years later, I have pretty much all the things I dreamt of. Two of my younger siblings live with me now, and I recently adopted my beautiful daughter. Though my partner and I are no longer together, we have a great relationship and we co-parent both our daughter and Laila. I do work I love. My life couldn't be more different from that fearful image I painted of myself dying in a hospital bed the day I tested positive.

In the last six years, I've probably shared my story with more than three thousand students. Each time, I tell them, I sat in the same Bay Area health class, in the same desks they're sitting in, learning about this stuff. I am not a bad person—you don't get HIV because you are a bad person. You can be a good person, an educated person, and get HIV. We have to get past the stigma—that is the reason people don't get tested and are not honest about their status.

This virus does not happen to people because they deserve it. By sharing my story, *that* is the legacy I want to leave behind.

Hearing each other's stories reminds us that we're all fighting the good fight, to show understanding and compassion for those who struggle, and that there's power when you surround yourself with good people. Laila gave me that. Whether it was the peaceful walks or nights she was there to lean on—she provided a home I could go back to, a place of reprieve. Laila showed me what unconditional love truly is. When humans were casting me out or saying hurtful things behind my back, Laila showed up for me— she was consistently loyal—and she still shows up for me. Every single day, she meets me with love.

Healing Each Other

BRAD & THOR

Before Thor, I was terrible at taking my HIV medication. I partied every night and sold drugs. I really didn't care about anything, and I didn't see any reason to change my lifestyle, even though it was slowly killing me.

One day a friend of mine asked me to help him find a home for a dog named Thor whose previous owner had been arrested numerous times for selling drugs. After he moved to the projects, Thor's owner would let his roommates use Thor in dogfights in return for free drugs. And when I met Thor, he was healing from a stab wound from a recent police raid. I didn't plan on keeping him, but as soon as he came into my house, he lay on his back to let me rub his belly and I could tell that he felt immediately comfortable with me.

Thor stayed with me for several weeks while I tried to find him a home. But as I looked, we grew closer and closer. One day I realized I had already found a home for him—mine. When I decided I was going to keep this dog, I knew I had to get serious about making changes to better my life. Not just for me, but because Thor deserved to live in a stable home.

If I was going to keep Thor in my life, I needed to make sure I wouldn't do anything that could cause him to be uprooted or harmed again. His previous owner was also a drug dealer like me and had been busted, which was what left Thor without a home and under my watch, so that meant I had to stop dealing as well. I couldn't stay out late anymore, because I needed to be home to take care of him. Bit by bit, through making adjustments to give Thor a safe and healthy home, I became healthier and safer in my own life. And, for the first time, I got clean.

If I hadn't met Thor, I wouldn't be here today. All of my friends are gone. None of them lived to see their thirties except for me, and I partied a lot harder and was headed down a more dangerous path than they were. But I somehow made it. That I'm still here today doesn't make a lot of sense. The only way I do make sense of it is by looking at Thor. My decision to care for him has given me reason to care for myself. I know that without him I wouldn't be alive, and without me he wouldn't either. We saved each other.

What the Universe Intended

SAMUS STARBODY & ZEUS

had just celebrated my twenty-first birthday when I went to the doctor for the checkup that changed my life. I still remember that moment so vividly. It was the Wednesday after Easter, April 3, 2013, and the nurse told me that my HIV test had come back positive. Everything went dark. I wanted to cry but couldn't. The clinic was almost an hour from where I went to school at the University of Illinois at Chicago. On the ride back, I tried to keep my mind blank for as long as possible so I wouldn't do something irrational. When I finally got to my dorm room, I broke down and spent the next week in bed, crying and sleeping.

I can't lie—I had been behaving badly. After a bad breakup months earlier, I had been yearning for attention. I told myself I was taking control of my sexuality and my body at the time, but the reality was that I had been acting irresponsible and reckless, and I knew that wasn't me. After my diagnosis I felt like I should've known better. I kept thinking, *Maybe if you had focused on your art, or on your friends, or expressed yourself a little bit more, then you might not have gotten this.*

The last month of my junior year was a blur. I came home for summer break depressed. I wasn't laughing as much. I wasn't enjoying the things I used to. I dressed differently, talked differently—I was just going through the motions. It was my dog, a Maltese poodle named Wynter I'd had since I was a sophomore in high school, who comforted me. While my sister was with her dad and my mom was at work, me and Wynter developed a closeness we didn't have before. I'd sit and talk to her, and she would stare into my eyes and listen to anything and everything. She wouldn't let me sleep for too long, but when I did go to sleep, I'd roll over to find her head on my pillow next to me. She understood that I was in pain. If I ever got upset, she'd lick my face or try to encourage me to go outside.

Before HIV, I rarely got sick and was used to running and dancing every day. I wasn't used to feeling weak and lethargic all the time. It was different when I was with Wynter, though. Every time I took her out, she was so excited that I couldn't help but be excited too. Her positivity was infectious. When I was feeling good, we would race and she would cut in front of me to stop me from winning, which made me laugh. No matter what I wanted to do or where I wanted to go, Wynter was beside me. She was almost like my nanny. Even though I was supposed to be taking care of her, she was taking care of me.

When I returned to school for my senior year, I was able to channel the frustration and anger over my HIV diagnosis into my work. I found a way to bring my art into my business classes, which I had previously dreaded but took because my parents pushed me to. Once I made that connection, I excelled and ended up having my most successful year in college.

Knowing I was sick and had to take medication every day was hard for me. My body did not take to the pills. I started getting patches of dry skin and couldn't be in the sun. If I took them even three minutes later than my scheduled time, I was in pain and eventually I decided to stop taking my medication altogether.

I went without medication for two years, and everything seemed fine. I got a job at Michaels art supply store and became their most decorated manager. Customers loved me because I loved them—I genuinely appreciated their business and speaking with them about art. Being on the move and helping people made me feel better about myself and took my mind off my condition. But I became a workaholic, trying to prove that I could still be at the top of the pack as I had been before HIV. When Michaels changed its corporate strategy and laid off their managers, including me, I felt lost again. At the same time, my family moved to a new house in a rougher neighborhood and Wynter couldn't run around as much. I could feel things were changing and she was slowing down.

The morning of my twenty-fourth birthday, my friend died in a car accident. After that loss, I connected with a mutual friend named Andre through our grief. He and I were both active people, so having to sit back and process what we were going through was uncomfortable, but that brought us closer together. Eventually we fell in love, and Wynter fell in love with Andre too. My goodness, sometimes she would pay more attention to him than to me! He cared for her like his daughter. He would research new recipes to make for her, and it got to the point where if he didn't feed her, she wouldn't eat. I was a little jealous, but I understood he was trying to care for and love on her the way he wished he could for the friend we lost.

It had been a stressful year, which was hard on my body. When we committed to each other, Andre pushed me to start taking my HIV medicine again and be more on top of my health. He took me to every doctor's appointment and read up on my medications and what I could and could not eat with them. As he became a more central part of my life, it felt like Wynter was passing the torch to him.

Occasionally, the pain we were both feeling would come out and we would lash out at each other. One morning we got into a fight and I decided to take Wynter with me for a walk. I didn't put on her leash like I usually do, because Andre had started training her to walk without one and she was good at it. Andre was much rougher when he disciplined Wynter on their off-leash walks, which bothered me. As we were walking that morning, she started to go into someone's yard. I reached for her, but she bolted like I was going to hit her. At that moment, a car was barreling down the street and they met in the intersection. She died right in front of my eyes.

One of the first thoughts I had when I tested positive was, "Am I going to be able to have kids?" Wynter had become my child. I carried her home, wailing at the top of my lungs. My family tried to console me, but I felt like a piece of my heart had died with her that day. For weeks, I'd come home expecting to find her barking on the other side of the door, and it hurt every time I was met with silence.

A month later, my cousin texted me. She had a greyhound puppy she couldn't keep, and she wanted to know if I would take him. I was apprehensive at first, having just gone through such a big loss, but my mom and sister pushed the idea. "This might be good for you," they said. Eventually I caved and met Zeus.

Zeus was extremely shy. I was used to Wynter, who would run down the street to try to get on the bus with me. The first night Zeus stayed with us we heard a loud squeak coming from a toy he was playing with. Andre and I turned around and Zeus, noticing he was caught, put his paws over his face to hide his embarrassment. It was adorable. After that, I understood him. He was silly, and he was going to be the one to make us laugh. The next day, officially attached to him, Andre and I brought him to the dog park. As soon as we let him off leash, he bolted. In that moment, the memory of Wynter came rushing back and my stomach dropped. I held my breath and willed myself to sit down, bracing myself to be hurt again. But when I looked up, there was Zeus, rushing back toward me.

Where Wynter provided the comfort and consistency I needed to overcome my HIV diagnosis, Zeus is an embodiment of new healthy relationships and embracing this next chapter of my life. If I thought that Wynter pushed me to get up and out, Zeus is on another level. When he's ready to go, he jumps on the bed to wake me up, and once we're outside he can run for hours. He loves riding in the car and going for hikes. Zeus pushes me to be more active and more disciplined—as a human and an artist. When *Art AIDS America*—an exhibition on how AIDS has affected the US—came to Chicago and they needed people to give tours, something told me it might be good for me. As I went through the works, I felt my story wasn't being represented, so I wrote poems connecting each piece on display to a different phase in my own journey with HIV. With every person who was willing to join my tour and listen, a weight was lifted—I felt I didn't have to hide anymore.

In hindsight, I feel like my HIV diagnosis was a way for the universe to tell me during a time of pain, "This is not the type of life you're meant to live." Since then, and with the help of Wynter and Zeus, it feels like I am finally realizing what the universe intended.

He Loves Me for Me

DENNIS & BUDDY

don't want to say there wasn't love in my household growing up, but it wasn't exhibited in a healthy way. I never had a great relationship with my parents. My mother harbored a lot of resentment toward my grandmother, who—when my mom got pregnant at sixteen—sent her away until she gave birth, then forced her to give the baby up for adoption. It seemed like that stunted her emotionally. She'd do anything to piss off my grandmother, including marrying my father and refusing to clean our home. I never had a playdate growing up because I was embarrassed by how unkempt the house was, and I developed a lot of insecurity around my ability to make friends. On a subconscious level, that created this belief that people wouldn't like me if they knew the real me.

Those early challenges with human relationships continued into adulthood and limited my ability to form friendships and intimacy. While searching for those connections, I turned to drug use and careless sexual relationships. So, I wish I could say that I was surprised when I tested positive for HIV in 1995, but I wasn't. By that time, I had moved from Chicago to New Jersey for a new job, and with almost no friends out there, I already felt lonely, tired and a little bit depressed. Once I was diagnosed, I especially wasn't up to putting myself out there to build friendships. I used shopping as a social crutch because I didn't like being alone. I would go to department stores once, if not twice a week, to talk to the salespeople and spend money on clothes—many of which still have the tags on them. I'm not going to lie—it was nice to always know what was on sale at Bloomingdale's, but unfortunately that was the entirety of my social life.

I started seeing a counselor to talk about my feelings around my HIV status and to get help opening up to new relationships. Since distancing myself from my family, I realized that love had never compelled me to take responsibility for anyone's well-being. That led me to first adopt a nine-year-old dachshund named Clive. He had been brought to a shelter by an older couple who could no longer take care of him. Clive was sweet and shied away from attention, unlike his brother in the next cage. When I took him out, he just sat on my lap and let me pet him. Clive was the perfect introduction to adopting a dog. So when he passed after three years together, I felt ready to adopt a three-month-old hound-beagle mix named Buddy, who I've had since. He's got a ton of energy. My friend and neighbor Mike adopted Buddy's shelter mate, Dexter, and the two became instant companions. I'd bring them to the dog park two or three times a week. When they'd get into the car, I'd roll the windows down and those boys could be heard from a block away as I was pulling up to the park. Everyone knew us there, and that helped me open up a bit.

The nature of having a dog is social. Everybody in my condo complex knows my dog and I know theirs. When I take Buddy out, I have more confidence when talking to people. At the end of the day, I am perfectly happy to spend the evening taking Buddy for a walk and relaxing at home, because I simply enjoy the time that I get to spend with him. When I come through the door, his tail is wagging. I pet him and hold him and scratch his belly. We play together. I pretend that I'm going to get his tail, and he freaks out—like, he actually thinks I'm going to take it. I experience every bit of joy in the world in moments like those.

It wasn't until after I adopted Buddy that I really understood how my upbringing has affected me. I equate the relationship I have with him to the relationship that a mother or father has with a child—in a way, he is my child. When I brought him home, I had this instinct to protect him from the toxic behavior that has caused me a lifelong struggle with shame, judgment and unworthiness. All my life I've wanted to do better and be better than what my parents created. I've wanted to grow and evolve to the best version of myself. The only way I could do that was by being willing to take a hard look at my family dynamics, as uncomfortable as it may be, and build a relationship with somebody who needed me.

I have been undetectable for ten years, and I credit a large part of my good health to the joy that I get from my dog. Buddy loves me for me. He is there for me and simply wants me to be happy. Animals don't judge one another because of the way they look or because of handicaps or cultural differences. There's no "Oh my god, he's got weird paws! Let's not be his friend." That lesson in radical acceptance and unconditional love has been invaluable for me, and I think it's a lesson that every one of us could afford to learn.

My complicated relationships with intimacy aren't entirely resolved, and I hope they are in time for me to enjoy a human-to-human relationship at some point in my life. But if it doesn't happen, that's okay too. I'm very happy with the one that's waiting for me every day when I come home.

My Stud, My Strength

PAULO & STUD

When I was seventeen, I was walking in New Orleans when I met two men who would change my life forever. After talking with them for a few minutes, they pulled me into a nearby alley and started roughing me up while yelling that they were going to give me AIDS. Eventually they pulled down my pants and raped me. Even today, I can still hear their voices shouting, "We're gonna give you AIDS! We're gonna give you AIDS!" over and over, rattling around in my head. I tested positive for HIV a few weeks later.

I grew up just over the bridge from New Orleans. I come from a conservative southern family, and my parents were not okay with me being gay. As a teenager, I was trying to find my place in the world and figure out who I was when I started sneaking out and going into the city in search of acceptance and community. Unfortunately, I found those things through drugs and sex. My parents didn't agree with my lifestyle, so I was emancipated from them at sixteen, and I started hooking and selling drugs to get by.

Every day that I struggled on my own and wasn't able to call my mom and hear her say, "I love you" was really difficult. For months after that night in New Orleans, the only way I knew how to cope with what had happened to me was denial. This led to a major downward spiral, during which I battled different addictions and health issues. The most difficult was my battle with meth, which became the cure and cause for everything good and bad in my life.

When Hurricane Katrina hit, my parents and I spoke a few hours before the electricity went out. The bridge that connects the city to where they live got destroyed, so I couldn't get back to see them. We weren't able to get in contact for nineteen days, because all the phone lines were down.

Displaced and with nowhere to go, I ended up in Chicago. The first winter I spent there I became incredibly sick. By the time I got to the hospital, my viral load was over a million and my T cells were at fourteen. When I realized how bad my health had gotten, I decided to go to Howard Brown Health Center to get my life together. There, in Chicago, I was able to get and stay sober for eight years.

That changed when my partner died. My grief was complicated, because he had been abusive to me for our entire relationship—physically, mentally and emotionally. I felt like he loved me every time he hit me in the face. I travel to do makeup for a living and would have to wear a full face of the cover-up I was selling to hide the bruises. Though he and I were both sober while we were together (as far as I knew), he relapsed while I was out of town on a work trip, and while he was high, he killed himself. Losing him was painful, but I also felt a strange relief because his death was a way out.

A few months after he passed, my mom was diagnosed with stage III lung cancer. I took a job in Atlanta to be closer to my parents, with whom I'd been mending a relationship since I got sober. But living in a new city where I knew no one, while battling grief and guilt over my partner and my mom's illness, I fell into a deep depression. The only way I knew how to manage my pain was with drugs, and—far from the sober support groups and community I had in Chicago—I relapsed and started dealing again.

Eventually I decided that I needed to do something to help myself get better, because for the first time I was feeling like I didn't want to wake up anymore. I needed something, or someone, to hold me accountable for my life and to remind me to travel lightly—to not get weighed down by the darkness surrounding me. Years earlier, I'd had a dog who was a big help to me in hard times. I thought maybe a dog could help me get through this too.

While searching for breeds, I came across a French bulldog described as "a clown in the cloak of a philosopher." That stuck with me. From growing up in a household where I was the rebel, the black sheep and "the colorful son" (as my mom used to call me), this dog embodied how I'd felt my entire life; I'd just never been able to put it into words.

Stud was from a breeder in Kentucky, and when I met him, I immediately felt myself become lighter. Every time I walked through the door, his tail was wagging and he was happy to see me. Stud was the first dog I got on my own, and caring for him gave me purpose. It took me out of myself and my selfish habits, and I started to see my life change for the better.

No matter what, every morning and evening I had to take Stud out for a walk. That responsibility forced me to maintain some connection to the outside world and other people. I developed a routine. With Stud getting me up earlier, I became more consistent about taking my HIV medication, which made me feel better physically. While we were out, people always seemed to want to talk to us and pet him, and that motivated me to present myself better. I started making an effort to get dressed and put myself together before we went out to the park, and slowly my confidence grew.

Though I was still dealing drugs, my life was starting to turn around and I could see a way out. Unfortunately, my last deal cost me my dog. En route to a client, I realized I was being followed. If I got caught, I'd go to jail, so I bailed. I flushed the drugs and checked into detox. Since I never brought my boss his money, he raided and robbed my apartment, and he took Stud with him. I've called countless times to try to strike a deal or reason with him to get my dog back, but he's a drug dealer deep in his own addiction—I know firsthand how that can impair your morals—and eventually he stopped answering my calls.

Losing Stud is one of the hardest things I've had to accept. While I'm grateful I got the chance to start over and build an honest, healthy life, my biggest regret is that I didn't get there until I lost Stud. He deserved more. I think about and miss him constantly, but I won't get another dog until I'm certain I can give him everything he deserves—that's the only way I can do right by Stud.

I always say meth gave me wings but took away the sky. Stud was the sky that gave me hope. He kept me present and eased the social anxiety I acquired after being attacked all those years ago. I frequently had trouble sleeping. Many nights, I would be up crying in bed and Stud would lick my tears. I felt safe when he was with me. In that dark place, Stud was the only source of light, and he became the path to some sort of healing—as complicated as that path ended up being.

Looking back, I think my addiction and lifestyle spiraled from the shame and guilt I felt around being HIV positive. Since then, I've grown and learned a lot about self-acceptance and love. Recently, a friend asked me whether I would take a pill to get rid of HIV if I could. To be honest, I wouldn't. I've had the virus my whole adult life—I don't know who I would be without it.

If I hadn't had him by my side, I probably wouldn't be alive today. For years, when my life seemed to be one hardship after another, it was Stud who gave me the strength to push on. I couldn't have passed up this opportunity to share our story. He truly saved me, and I hope that this will bring someone hope.

Everyone Needs a Little Couture

MICHELLE, RAVEN & COUTURE

Michelle (*left*) and
Raven with Couture

My mom didn't find out she was HIV positive until after I was born.

I was always very sick as a baby, and my mom began to get worried. She took me to the doctor and learned that I had become HIV positive, not through birth but from breastfeeding. I was no more than five years old when my mom told me I was sick. The first thing I said was, "Mommy, am I going to die?"

It was really hard living with HIV as a child. I was open about my status, and I faced a lot of stigma at school because of it. I was bullied—the other kids wouldn't even let me use the bathroom—and teachers wouldn't let me go on class trips out of fear. I never told my mom, but she eventually found out and transferred me to a new school. "We are going to be survivors," she said. And I've remembered that ever since.

Shortly after that she got me a dog named Charlie, and he brought me so much joy. He was the only one in the world I could talk to about everything going on at school and in my life, and he was such a good listener. He would even lie with me when I cried at night. Charlie wasn't just my best friend, he was my only friend for a long time. When Charlie died, I was a teenager. We had just moved to Brooklyn, and it was there that I began to really come into my own, with my mom's help.

I fell in love when I was nineteen. I disclosed my status to him, and he totally accepted it. For the first time in my life I felt the weight of that stigma lift off my shoulders, and I let myself fall into the arms of love. We were together for six years, and not only did I love him, but my mother did too. He was one of the first men in both of our lives who loved us unconditionally, despite our HIV status, and he didn't hurt me like my father hurt my mother when I was younger.

One Valentine's Day, my boyfriend woke me up and said, "You want a dog?" At the time, our relationship was rocky. While my boyfriend was okay with my status, his family was deeply against him dating someone who was HIV positive, and that began to destroy our relationship. I think getting a puppy was his final attempt to salvage it.

We got up that morning, he took me to a pet store, and that's where I got Couture. From the moment I saw her, I knew she was something special. She reminded me of the kindness I was missing in my relationship, even though we were trying our best. I named her Couture because to me, she was suddenly the most valuable thing in my life.

My boyfriend and I broke up shortly after I got Couture, and I was devastated. Our whole family was devastated. While I knew he loved me and wanted to be with me, that wasn't enough to fight off the tremendous stigma surrounding HIV.

I am still grateful for our relationship and for Couture, who has given me what Charlie did when I was a child: unconditional love. The love of a dog is something even more special than couture, and even stronger than stigma.

From Nobody to Somebody

STEVEN & GAV

t was 1985, shortly after I turned twenty-three, when I went to see the doctor for a minor cold. He told me that the HIV test had just come out on the market and recommended that all of his gay patients take the test.

At the time I was wary about it. HIV was still being called gay-related immunodeficiency, or GRID, and the most I had heard about it was from a headline on the cover of a gay Chicago bar guide that mentioned some kind of new cancer affecting gay men. I didn't know anyone who had been personally impacted by the disease, and no one in Chicago was really talking about it. It was still a relatively minor story.

Ultimately, I agreed to take the test at my doctor's insistence. It was nothing like the rapid tests that clinics provide today. In the eighties, it took three weeks to get your results. When mine finally came back, my doctor told me I had tested positive and that I had eighteen months to live. I could barely process those words. All of these thoughts started racing through my head: *I will never see twenty-five; I will never see the year 2000.* I found myself mourning for the future—a future I didn't even know—because death was suddenly so imminent.

Then eighteen months came and went, and there wasn't so much as a hiccup with regard to my health. In that time, some of my friends became sick. Some had died. News of the "gay cancer"—eventually dubbed human immunodeficiency virus, or HIV—grew bigger and more urgent and, for far too many, more deadly. People began talking about it. In many ways it felt like it was consuming or destroying the gay community. So, shortly after testing positive, I decided to drop out of school and travel the world. If I could die tomorrow, I thought, why waste my precious time working toward any long-term goals like earning a college degree.

High-profile cases of HIV-positive individuals emerged. I watched with America as Hollywood actor Rock Hudson chartered planes to Paris for experimental treatments. Ryan White—an innocent thirteen-year-old hemophiliac who contracted the virus through lifesaving blood transfusions—had won the love of the world and died anyway. I thought, *How was I, a nobody from the South Side of Chicago, going to survive this if they couldn't?*

But I *was* surviving, and for years, things were going well. As I got older, reports came out about the effects of HIV medications on the aging process, and I became stressed out again. People were starting to have health problems after being on the antiretroviral pills for so long. Reports were suggesting that if I stayed on these medications, my body would begin aging prematurely. I could no longer deal with the uncertainty over which day might be my last, so I started drinking to cope with my fears. Things continued to go well on my HIV medications—it was the drinking that became a problem. A big one.

My husband watched as I tried to drown my worries over my health and HIV status. Eventually he brought home Gav, in hopes that a dog might pull me out of my drinking problem. Just four months after Gav joined our family, I ended up in the hospital and went to rehab. However, once I got home from treatment, Gav became central to my recovery. Every day, Gav was there—a constant force of love and motivation. He gave me something else to focus on, to look forward to, to care for and, most importantly, to deter me from relapsing. And it helped. There have been many times when Gav has been the only one I could talk to without judgment, the only one I felt I could trust to always be there.

Caring for Gav helped me see that it's senseless to waste my days worrying. None of us knows which day will be our last. His pure excitement when I come through the door, his joy over the simplest things and the present moment has motivated me to make each day matter. Since Gav came into my life, I've decided to stop worrying about the time I might not have and start cherishing the time that I do.

Building Safe Spaces

CÉSAR, HOA, CHICO, PEPE & ANN

Hoa (*left*) and César
with Chico and Pepe

W e met at a club in San Francisco. César was working with an HIV organization conducting outreach, and Hoa was one of the volunteers. That was twenty-three years ago.

CÉSAR

I moved to San Francisco when I was twenty-one to discover the world and find the community that—as a young gay man growing up in Hawaii—I was missing. It was 1984, and San Francisco was ground zero for the growing AIDS crisis. Though we didn't understand what that meant just yet, there was this mindset, born out of stigma, that if you were gay, you were going to end up with the virus.

When I was diagnosed with HIV in 1989, death felt inevitable. All around me, people were dying—often just two weeks or a month after being diagnosed. To make matters worse, they were dying very painful, stigmatized and extremely visible deaths, whether because of extreme weight loss or Kaposi's sarcoma. Why would I be any different? There weren't a lot of role models, because fear and stigma kept people from speaking openly. This was especially true among the Asian community, where historically people have avoided talking about fatal diseases because it might generate energy around it happening. Families said their sons died from pneumonia because they feared putting the real cause of death on their burial plots.

I tried my best to be healthy, to take care of myself and stay alive. As weeks turned into months and I was still around, I started to think, *Maybe I can hope.* Those of us who were surviving came together to build a safe space, where we could be out and support each other. We could talk about our fears and how we felt. That helped me learn to take care of myself through those early years, when I wasn't getting support from my family.

For the first five years I was in San Francisco, I didn't talk to my family about my personal life because I was afraid of being disowned. Before I left home, I'd had a negative experience after being caught dating a guy, and none of my family members stood up for me. After that, I became wary about how people would respond to my sexuality and status. I didn't come out to them until '93. By then, I knew that as a gay, Asian and HIV-positive man, I deserve respect, love and happiness like everybody else. I wanted my family in my life, but they needed to know who I was.

In 1998, I returned to Hawaii to take a job as the executive director of the Kauai AIDS Project. It would be good for my career and, since I was from Hawaii, I thought I could be effective. What I didn't anticipate was the difference in culture. In San Francisco, I had spoken openly about my status and found support and acceptance. Moving from there to Kauai—which is smaller and even more rural than where I grew up—I felt like I was stepping back in time to the Hawaii I had left all those years ago. There was still stigma, shame and fear surrounding HIV, and everyone on the island knew each other.

Among the gay community, many of the men were clients of the AIDS project, so as the executive director I felt I needed to maintain professional boundaries even when it came to personal relationships. But that left me isolated. That's when I got Pepe and Chico. Having dogs at home broke down that loneliness. Knowing I was strong enough to build a family helped me to want to continue to be healthy

HOA

When I met César in San Francisco, we both had our own things going on—he was taking a job in Hawaii and I was starting a graduate program in LA. Plus, there is an eleven-year age gap between us, so we were at different points in our lives. We lived apart for the first five to six years after we met and continued to build a relationship in spite of the distance.

In grad school, I was studying public health—I wanted to understand the discrimination and injustice in our institutions and make it easier for people to get healthy through public resources. I've always believed in promoting prevention rather than treatment and got tested every six months, so when I was diagnosed with HIV in 2004 I was disappointed in myself. I was fortunate that, unlike César fifteen years earlier, when I received my diagnosis I felt safe to talk about it. By that time, César and I were living together in Pasadena with Chico and Pepe, and it was really helpful to come home to their unconditional love and support. César and his friends who are positive were my role models; they reassured me I could live a healthy life.

I didn't tell my family directly. Coming out as gay had been a challenge. When I tried to tell my mom, she didn't understand what I was trying to say because of our language barrier (I am first-generation Chinese American). She pulled my sister into the room, and she tried to explain that it was a phase. Then she called my brother in, who tried to talk to me about my "choice." I had to explain to the three of them that this was not a choice or a phase. They've been supportive since, but it's typical of Asian families to be concerned with saving face and they do not want to hear your dirty laundry. They ask how I'm feeling, but otherwise we don't talk about health issues unless it's a dire situation.

In recent years, my involvement with the AIDS Ride has forced me to be open about my story, so I think they are aware of my status. I am glad that they can see I am not taking this diagnosis lightly—I take my health seriously and help those who continue to suffer. Today, I see HIV as a blessing in disguise. My body tells me I'm not invincible and that I have to be proactive about taking care of myself.

My mom passed away in 2006. Soon afterward, a stray dog showed up at our door. We shooed her away, but she wouldn't leave. She had no tags, so we put lost-dog signs throughout the neighborhood. But no one claimed her, which was unusual. She was a pure white Pomeranian puppy, still teething, and we lived in an Asian community where that is a popular breed. Pomeranian was my mom's favorite kind of dog. After unsuccessfully trying to find the dog's owner, we took it as a sign that my mom wanted her to be with us, so we named her after my mom, Ann.

US

We both come from large families. César has seven siblings and Hoa has twelve. Needless to say, it is very important to both of us to live in an environment where beings are dependent on one another for love and support. Chico, Pepe and Ann helped us create that. Being able to build a home with them made us feel whole—they are our family.

Having dogs connected us with our neighbors, many of whom are dog owners, and through them we got involved in a program for fostering older dogs—extending our family even further. In the last couple years, we've fostered twenty-two senior dogs. These are dogs that no one else wants—they've been abandoned, found on freeways and are going to be euthanized. Some have been blind, deaf or missing limbs. And yet, when they come into our home and realize they're safe, their personalities start to come out. Soon they run around and play like the rest of the dogs—all because they were given the attention and care all living creatures deserve. It gives us purpose to know we have the means to provide that, and it reminds us that if one day we are unwell and need help, we too can reach out to others for support.

For us, dogs have been a symbol of resilience. They've shown us that regardless of age and health condition, if you build a positive, loving environment, you can live a happy life and even thrive. That's such a life-affirming message. Having dogs has shown us that HIV is not a burden. Rather, it is a reminder that we have limited time in this life and it challenges us to do something with it—not only to better ourselves but also to better those around us.

A Bridge to Healing

HARLEY & CELIE

By the time I moved to Los Angeles at age twenty-nine, I thought nothing could scare me because of what I'd already been through.

I'd been on my own since I was fifteen—the same age my mother was when she had me. We moved around a lot, and were never surrounded by any sort of extended family who could help provide stability or support. When I was a sophomore in high school, my mom wanted to move again. I was excelling in performing arts at my high school and didn't want to leave and start over, so I decided to move out. As I bounced around between the homes of teachers and friends, I started getting anxiety attacks from the unresolved stress of being displaced at a young age. But I made it.

After high school I left for California to pursue a music career but didn't know anyone out there. Feeling isolated and depressed, I surrounded myself with questionable people, so I wasn't surprised when I found out I was HIV positive in 2014. My so-called friends soon disappeared. I didn't want to be alone, so I got Celie in August and named her after the main character in *The Color Purple*, because that story is about survival and strength and I knew I would need the constant reminder.

As if my diagnosis wasn't enough, a short time into treatment I started experiencing other health issues—fainting spells, tremors and problems with my memory. I would forget to take my HIV medication. That's when I started teaching Celie little tricks to help me. Every morning at nine she went to the basket where I kept my medication and grabbed the bottle I needed, opened the mini fridge and removed a bottle of water and brought them to me. She would then sit and wait until I took the pills. If I didn't, she would bark. Training her to do that was as good for my physical health as it was for my mental health. Dogs are a direct representation of their owners, so her ability to learn reminded me that I was smart and strong when I needed it most.

For the next year and a half, my health gradually became worse. My doctor kept telling me I was depressed and not taking care of myself, but that didn't feel right. A seizure brought me to Cedars-Sinai, where the doctors discovered I had neurosyphilis, which had advanced significantly because of my HIV and because it had gone untreated. I would later find out that syphilis had shown up in my blood work three times before it progressed to my brain, and my doctor never even told me once.

By that point I was really, really sick. I'd also developed shingles and could barely move my legs. I lost my job as a server at a West Hollywood nightclub because I had to miss so much work. At the same time, my landlord raised my rent. Facing eviction, I sought out a public law office. They tried to extend my lease until they could find me a place to live, but we ran out of time. Unfortunately, Celie and I would end up spending more than a year living on the street.

Most shelters wouldn't allow dogs, and I wasn't going to be separated from Celie—she was the only stability I had. When churches served free soup, we would go there. I always made sure Celie had food even when I couldn't eat. With just $200 per month coming from a homeless stipend, I couldn't afford to stay in LA. I made my way to Palm Springs, where off-season I could afford a night or two at a cheap motel for just $30.

I knew that my biological father lived in California and had two daughters younger than me. We had spoken before and I really wanted to have a relationship with them, but the timing was difficult. When I ran out of money in Palm Springs, I called one of those half sisters who lived thirty miles away. I didn't want to ask for help outright, so I asked her, "Where do you go when you're sick?"

She said, "I go home." My heart sank.

I said, "Well, where am *I* supposed to go?" I hoped she would say that she'd come get me, but she didn't. She was young, and it was a lot to take in: a new sibling with HIV, and homeless, with a dog. Many people don't understand that not everyone has a home to go back to.

A few times, I'd get a call from my social worker if she thought she might have an apartment for us. I'd scrape together whatever money I could get to catch the shuttle back to LA, only to find that the place had fallen through. We'd stay on the streets in North Hollywood, where we could hide behind a bush and get some sleep. If I was afraid to sleep on the street, we might end up with tweakers who were up all hours of the night.

This all made me sink deeper into depression. It seemed like everyone was giving up on me. The government support I was supposed to get, the doctors, my family—they were all failing me. But not Celie. If I broke down crying, she would sit and stare at me as if to say, *You're going to be fine. We're in this together.*

Survival mode had become normal for me. I'd faced so many things in my life that I thought I had to be pretty dang tough. But living on the streets was scary. Luckily, Celie turned out to be a great defensive weapon. Pugs are so goofy-looking—I've watched the toughest people turn to pudding when they see her. That's when I first started to see how Celie could bring relief to others.

Once we were at a crosswalk in Hollywood waiting for the light to change, and this lady was talking on her cell phone, crying and frustrated. She slammed down her phone, buried her face into her hands and fell apart. Celie walked over to the woman and sat by her foot, staring at her. When the lady lifted her head and saw Celie, she slowly knelt down. Celie put her chin on the woman's knee and let her pet her head. When the light changed, she stood up and said to me, "You don't understand how much that just helped me." I thought, *Trust me, I do.* I collected every one of those interactions like bread crumbs to get back to the light.

There comes a time when you're so sick of suffering that something ignites in you to turn everything around. You can call it God, the divine, whatever you want—but when it happens, you start seeing things differently. All the darkness weighing on you starts to fall away. When I realized there was nothing else I could do to get help from others, the only thing left was to sit and heal myself.

On my walks with Celie, I found meditation. In Palm Springs, we'd spend hours walking. When we were both tired, I would find somewhere quiet to sit and just focus on my breathing. I felt the wind on my skin and a stillness, like I was frozen in time. I realized there was something there. I started trying to do it every day. It became my rock, my connection to something greater.

Though my mental health was improving, my physical health was not. My social worker could only get me medication if I was in LA County. She mailed me enough to last a few months in Palm Springs, but right before Christmas I ran out—I went without HIV medication and antidepressants for seven months, and there was nothing I could do. I ended up having a stroke, which put me in the hospital for eight days. Fortunately, someone I knew from Minnesota was on vacation in LA and got in touch. He rented a car and drove us back to Minneapolis where I got back on my feet.

A little more than a year ago, my last MRI brain scan was completely clear. My health is phenomenal, I am on my HIV meds and undetectable and I don't take antidepressants anymore. Meditation continues to be a daily practice for me, and I've even started to teach meditation and host talks on trauma and healing. I feel the greatest I've ever felt. I just moved in with a dear friend and feel like I am finally embarking on a new life, starting a new journey.

Celie has helped me see that your past doesn't determine your future. All the crap I've been through helped inform my path to heal others. During our year on the streets, Celie was a bridge to people who sometimes didn't want to connect. She got them to open up. I believe a lot of the stigma surrounding HIV comes from feeling like you can't be open about your status because someone's going to look at you differently. HIV is part of my story, and the more honest I've become about sharing it, the more people have been receptive.

Celie is also a reminder that love is healing. She showed me the power of empathy, compassion and connection. Through everything, she never left my side, never stopped reminding me that I am a good person. There's going to come a time when Celie will have been in my life longer than my mother was. It's from an unexpected source, but I'm grateful to finally be getting those lessons on unconditional love and stability that I wasn't able to get growing up.

My Comfort after the Dark

SHARON & DULK

t wasn't nice the way the doctor told me I was HIV positive, and for a long time it put me in a really dark place.

I tested positive in 1996. I had been sick—like, *really* sick—for weeks, but I thought I just had a bad cold. On a trip to Santa Barbara to surprise my mom for Mother's Day, my cough had gotten worse. As soon as I arrived in California, my mother took one look at me and knew something was seriously wrong. I was ninety-eight pounds and had a nasty cough that wouldn't stop. She drove me straight to the emergency room.

I was quickly admitted to the hospital that day. The doctors promptly moved me into the intensive care unit and ran all sorts of tests. After several hours, a doctor came to the door and blurted out, "You have AIDS, and you have six months to live. You need to get your affairs in order." My family tried to ask questions about treatment and options, but the doctor said there was nothing else they could do. He turned around and walked out, and everyone burst into tears. I sat there in silence, trying to remain composed and taking it all in.

I slowly recovered and was eventually well enough to be discharged from the hospital, but in the weeks after I was released my life started to unravel. I lost my house, my car and my job in Washington, DC. As soon as I'd heard those words, "You have AIDS"—and that I was going to die in six months—I couldn't muster the strength to do anything. And when you do nothing, you have nothing.

I spent months in a downward spiral and depressive slump, holed up in a dark room, scared, crying and alone. My family didn't know what to do, and no one knew what to tell my six-year-old son. After six months of watching me wallow, my mom barged into my room one day and gave me a wakeup call. "You have a son out there," she said. "You need to make up your mind whether you're going to live or die. If you're going to lie here and die like the doctor said, you can't do it here. You need to get up and brush yourself off and get on with living."

It took a few days for my mom's words to really sink in, but in the end, I chose not to die. I chose to live. I went to see a different doctor. I started HIV treatment, and over time I grew healthier and stronger, at least physically. But inside, I still struggled with depression and felt like I was still trapped in that dark room. The stigma and shame of being HIV positive was overwhelmingly isolating.

One day, my sister went to an animal shelter and adopted Dulk. From the moment she brought him home to me, he never missed a beat. Dulk became the thing I'd needed most since my diagnosis: a companion. Most people don't know about my status. Other than when I give educational talks at a school, my HIV diagnosis is something I have kept to myself. Over the years, Dulk has been my sole friend. He has been the confidant with whom I hold nothing back. With him, I can be completely myself. All he wants is to give unconditional love and be loved in return. That's all I want too. He is attuned to me and my needs. When I'm not feeling well, he lies next to me and puts his head in my lap while I watch TV and rest.

There are times when I still get lonely, and I don't know if that will ever go away completely. I worry it will be hard to find someone who will accept me and look past the stigma associated with HIV. But I am hopeful because I have Dulk. I am not worried that I'm going to lose him over something insignificant or silly. Every day, his unwavering love is a reminder of why I decided to live, to leave that dark room and face the light again. With Dulk, the dark doesn't scare me much anymore.

When Dogs Heal

Someone to Belong To

DANIEL & LOKI

'm from Chicago, from a very large Latin family. As the youngest of seven—I have five brothers and a sister—there were a lot of expectations for who I would become. Coming out was difficult. I was outed by my brother when I was sixteen, and it wasn't accepted. Because of that I never had a chance to be close to my siblings.

My relationship with my family has informed everything that I do. Throughout my life, I've struggled to find acceptance, belonging and home. I spent my twenties battling those impulses while trying to finish school and have a life. Though I wasn't fully aware of it at the time, deep down I knew something was missing in my life. Unfortunately, I used substances to mask my feelings and fill that void.

One of the pitfalls of growing up young and gay in an urban environment is easy access to drugs and alcohol.

There, in my subset of the gay community, I found a family I never felt I had with my own. During that time I was working at a nightclub and pulling late hours. I'd lost sight of my future and dropped out of school. I used everything from marijuana to methamphetamine for relief, for belonging or sometimes just for escape.

In my late twenties I found out I had HIV. I was shell-shocked. When I got that diagnosis, I was flooded with loneliness and the feeling that no one was ever going to love me. It didn't help that my family wasn't a support system. They are aware of my diagnosis, but like most things, it's not something we discuss. They've never asked me anything about it. Some Latin families are like that—expressive but not communicative. It bothers me, of course, but that is what it is.

I buried my feelings about my diagnosis for a long time, locked them in some corner of my mind. Looking back on it now, though, I can see that all of this created the perfect storm that led me to Loki.

It was around my thirtieth birthday and just after I'd decided to get clean. My road to recovery had been very lonely. I lost a lot of friends. It's ironic that getting clean was my low. Loki was three months old and the last of the litter, like me. I had never really taken care of anything before. I had never really *loved* anything before. All of a sudden, coming home at 6 a.m. meant coming home to this adorable puppy crying his eyes out. At that moment, I thought, *I need to change my life.*

Dogs demand more of you. Whether you're taking care of yourself or not, their needs come first, and through that you end up putting yourself first. It's almost a mystical relationship—especially when you get a dog during a major transition in your life. Loki gave me a sense of home, safety and comfort that I desperately needed. As corny as it sounds, I felt like I finally had a home because he was there, and that really did change my life. Within six months, I went back to finish my degree at DePaul University, and over the next two to three years I got a bachelor's degree in advertising.

Today, Loki and I are inseparable. People say he's a lot like me. He's in sync with my emotions. When he runs up to people, his energy is like, *Love me, love me, love me!* I like to think I'm not like that, but I probably am—dogs are extensions of us. I think I'm overly affectionate because my family never was. I know my family loves me, but with people sometimes what's given isn't always what's received. It's not that way with a dog. A dog gives and shows love unconditionally. That's no small thing when a part of you fears you're unlovable.

Even my family can see the change in me. They love Loki because they feel he righted me—he rescued me from a dark place. They're almost nicer to the dog than they are to me. But that's okay, because I think that's the way that they show they care—they don't necessarily show affection to me, but they do to the extension of me. In that way, Loki has brought us closer together—especially with my father. He and I used to have no relationship, but he loves that dog. When my parents dog-sit, Loki sleeps in bed with my dad at night. I've noticed as my father's gotten older, his tough exterior has fallen away a bit and it's easier to have a connection. In turn, I've learned to forgive and have patience with him—a dog teaches you a *lot* of patience. Now I simply try to understand and accept my father for who he is. I haven't gotten there with my brothers yet, but I'm hopeful.

In the meantime, I've managed to make my own family with Loki. In caring for him, I've become more comfortable with who I am and what I can provide. A dog put me at ease a bit, helped me find my own self-worth. He's shown me acceptance and love in a way I've never known before, and I've tried to mirror that in other parts of my life— whether in my commitment to work, in my relationships with family and in the Ride for AIDS Chicago, through which I've made friends who taught me to be okay with my diagnosis. And Loki is central to all of that.

The ten years I've had Loki have been years of constant growth and evolution. He's made me aware of my tendencies and behaviors. I've stayed clean and barely even drink now, because I know it creates volatile emotions within me. I have learned to lead a different kind of life, and I know now that there are many other kinds of pleasures. Loki is really a symbol for me—a symbol of hope, of promise, of a future.

The Whole Me

JULIAN & PAPI

n 2007, my sister came home from military service with a parting gift from a good friend in her company—a miniature pinscher named Papi. At the time, I was in high school in the suburbs of Chicago and just starting to figure myself out.

I came out as gay early on and was bullied because of it. I had a small group of friends but was still somewhat of an outcast. I've always felt more comfortable by myself, even at home. My family is wonderful, and we love each other, but we don't really share details about our personal lives. Most of my conversations with my parents are about surface-level stuff like my health or finances. I keep my dating life to myself, and the only people in my family who know about my HIV status are my two older sisters. Papi was the only one who I felt I could be myself around.

I was diagnosed with HIV the summer after I graduated from high school. That changed everything. I had been getting tested every six months since I became sexually active, as my doctor recommended. I hadn't shown any symptoms of a sexually transmitted infection, so when, after a routine test, the doctor said he wanted to have me come back in to talk, I suspected it might be HIV. Still, the moment he told me I tested positive was a shock. As far as I knew, I hadn't slept with anyone who was positive.

Facing my diagnosis was scary. I wasn't super educated about HIV or safe sex up to that point. My parents did their best to teach us, but they were uneducated in that space too. They gave my sisters and me a brief birds-and-the-bees talk when I was ten or eleven and my sisters were in high school, but we never spoke about the risk of STIs or anything like that. My high school dedicated a day or two to sex ed, but I barely remember what we discussed. Once I became sexually active, I basically had to educate myself. I had a lot of fear and shame surrounding HIV, so when I tested positive it was kind of a whirlwind. I had to adjust both physically and mentally to taking medication every day, several times a day. At first, my stomach didn't take it well and I constantly felt bloated. I was depressed, fatigued and I lost weight.

Papi offered a distraction from all of that. For a while, I was afraid to tell anyone about my diagnosis, so he was the only one I could lean on. When I'd come home after a long day of class or work, I would talk to him about what had happened that day and what I was feeling, and we'd cuddle. When I had a day off, we would go to the park or to the Riverwalk, take a stroll or a hike and enjoy being in nature. If I was depressed, those outings would keep me focused and active. On days I was sick and had to stay in bed, Papi would sit at my feet. Whenever someone came towards my room, he would jump in front of me and stand at attention. Even though I knew it was just family coming to check on me, that hit a soft spot. Knowing that he was ready to protect me made me feel safe. Even though I was going through something difficult, I wasn't going through it alone.

Having Papi to talk to also helped me practice vocalizing my experience. As I became more comfortable speaking about it, I started being able to open up to others about my status. I met and connected with other HIV-positive people who introduced me to LGBT-focused services in Chicago, where I got help and resources for learning to live with my diagnosis. The more educated I became, the more I started to accept myself and this new part of my identity. I've become more open to participating in projects like *When Dogs Heal* and research studies focused on HIV prevention. I've educated some of my friends who, like me, didn't know much about the reality of contracting HIV or what it's like to live with the virus. On dating apps, like Scruff and Grindr, I am open about my status now. I like to think that even those small gestures help lessen the stigma out there.

Eventually I started dating again, and I met someone who was negative. Though it didn't ultimately work out between us, it wasn't because I was positive. It may sound simple, but that experience—dating without HIV being a central conflict—was important to my growth. It changed how I see myself as an HIV-positive person. I could be an advocate and be open about my status without letting it define me.

I don't think I would be the same person I am now if I had never gotten this diagnosis. HIV has changed a lot of things in my life for the better. It has changed my perspective on sex—that it just takes one time—and helped me prioritize self-care. Before I was diagnosed, I ate Taco Bell and McDonald's all the time. Now I eat better and exercise more. I take more walks with Papi because I understand how it affects my health.

Sometimes I worry I'm a hypocrite for saying I've accepted my HIV status when I still haven't told my parents. I've gone back and forth about that decision a lot over the years. At times it's bothered me that they don't know, but ultimately I feel that if I were to tell them it would add more stress to their lives, and I don't want to worry them because I am healthy and safe. But it's not off the table for the future.

In the meantime, I have Papi, who has been my best friend and my family through it all. I don't think I would have turned out the same without him. His love and support helped me see that my status can be a part of me, without it being the only or the first thing about me.

The Caretaker

CHRIS & BLAKELY

became HIV positive in the midst of an obstacle course. I had just moved to Los Angeles, and I decided to take part in the Zombie Run, an event where people dress like zombies and run through obstacles. I was in my element—it was fun and physical and everyone around me was having a good time.

While running, I began to feel terribly ill, but I was so dedicated to completing the course that I pushed through to the finish line. When I got there, I collapsed. I was rushed to the hospital with a 109-degree fever, pneumonia, dehydration and shingles. I didn't know it at the time, but I was seroconverting. In the hospital, all I could think about was my dog, Blakely, and if he was okay. I wasn't even worried about my own well-being.

After I left the hospital, I got tested at the Los Angeles Gay and Lesbian Center, where I learned I was HIV positive. To everyone's surprise, I wasn't even shocked by this. My non-reaction actually worried my HIV counselor so much that I was flagged for suicide ideation. During the following weeks, while I was recovering from the initial illness associated with seroconverting, Blakely sat calmly by my side. His usual high-energy demeanor was subdued. It was as though once I became sick, he seemed to know he had to take care of me.

I have been positive just a short while, and since my diagnosis I've started to jokingly call Blakely my husband because he has become my primary source of emotional support, and I am happy with that.

Recently, a meth addict attacked me while I was walking home and I suffered a few wounds. When Blakely saw them he came over and started to lick me, caring for me just as he did when I came home from the hospital after the race.

Through all of this, I have come to realize that the reason I wasn't worried when I found out I was HIV positive was because I had Blakely. I knew that not even HIV could change our bond, our love for each other. We keep each other safe no matter what.

The Power of Hope

STEVEN & HOPE

On April 21, 2006, I was sitting in my veterinarian's waiting room with my beloved boxer, Buster Brown, who had to be put down. Out of nowhere, a woman came in with her own boxer, who was pregnant and in labor but had suddenly stopped having contractions. The veterinarian scrambled to perform an emergency C-section to save the puppies. The office was tremendously understaffed, and she had no option but to turn to those of us in the waiting room. "I need help!" she shouted, while handing out rubber gloves.

The vet then turned to me and said, "Steven, you're up first."

That's how I met Hope. She was the third puppy out—so tiny and so sweet. It didn't look like she would make it because her breathing had stopped. Sensing the worry on my face, the vet said, "Just mimic what I'm doing," as she demonstrated the required compression to get the puppies breathing after their traumatic birth. I literally had to shake the life into this fragile little dog. When her mouth finally opened and she stuck out her tongue, the room was in tears.

Buster Brown was sitting nearby, watching me the entire time. Once the commotion had passed, I had to regain my composure and do what I had initially come for—let him go.

It was only one year earlier that I had lost my long-term partner to liver cancer. Buster Brown had been a huge source of support for me as I struggled to deal with that loss and pain. I don't think I could have gotten through that pain without him by my side. In a cruel twist of fate, Buster Brown then developed his own inoperable, cancerous tumor, which quickly diminished his quality of life. That day in the vet's office, I knew what I had to do to relieve his suffering. It was one of the hardest decisions of my life, but it was the right and merciful one. After Buster Brown was euthanized, everyone in the waiting room that day agreed that the timing felt like a sign. They encouraged me to adopt the puppy I had just helped bring back to life. My first reaction was that I wasn't ready. It was too soon. The loss was still so fresh, I couldn't imagine replacing Buster Brown with another dog.

Maybe it was the fear of facing grief alone, or maybe it was some kind of higher power—but somehow, some way, seven weeks later I reversed course and decided to take the newborn pup. I named her Hope.

My health has been up and down ever since I was diagnosed with HIV in 1989. When I tested positive, I was thirty-two years old, living in Boston and completely lost. I wasn't *surprised* exactly—I had been in all the wrong places at all the wrong times— but I was still in shock. Walking home from the clinic that day, I felt like I had left my body, a body that had failed me. I had watched many friends and acquaintances die during the AIDS epidemic, and all I could think was, *Now it's my turn.*

At first, I tried to resume the life I'd had before, but in a few years my health started failing. My T-cell count got extremely low, and I started losing weight and getting opportunistic infections. Fortunately, protease inhibitors had just come to market and those kept me healthy enough through the mid-2000s.

When I lost my then partner in 2004 to liver cancer, the stress and grief were so hard on my body I feel it paved the way for my own HIV-related cancer diagnosis the following year. At the time, I was too weak to undergo chemotherapy and radiation, so the doctors just removed the tumor, knowing it would likely come back. When it did—almost two years later, to the date—they told me I would have to endure chemotherapy and thirty days of radiation. Without my partner, and without Buster Brown, I was afraid. I felt abandoned and alone, and I started to further close myself off from others. It was Hope who pulled me out of it.

She had come into my life just a couple months earlier—the timing couldn't have been more fortuitous. When I needed her most, Hope quickly became my focus to keep going forward.

The first few months were rough, because she was a rambunctious puppy and I didn't have the energy to keep up with her. I felt guilty that I couldn't be the dog parent she deserved and considered putting her up for adoption. Thank God I didn't. Instead, I sent her to a professional trainer who helped Hope get certified as a service animal. From then on, she never left my side.

Hope knew I was sick. From the beginning, she was cautious and protective of me. She would lie on my bed keeping watch every day as I returned from round after round of radiation therapy. There were times that I had to keep her out of the room because of the radiation in my system, and she would just lie at the door and wait. One day in particular, I was feeling so nauseated that I locked her out of my bedroom and put my headphones on to try to drown everything out and meditate. Hope was so anxious she chewed a hole through the door trying to get to me.

Every night she would follow me into bed and snuggle with me, and it was such an amazing comfort. She just always knew, you know?

Once I realized the deep connection we were establishing, I no longer felt alone. With Hope, I had the tightest bond I'd felt with an animal in my life—we were almost telepathic. When my father passed away in 2010, Hope and I were living in San Francisco with my current partner, Michael. There were times when I'd sit upstairs alone, crying, and Hope would suddenly appear and start licking the tears off my face. She was incredibly in tune with my emotions.

Without Hope, I would have stayed cooped up, alone and isolated. But with her, I went everywhere—from the park to shops to airplanes. On our walks, we strolled past the neighborhood gay bars and restaurants. Everyone in the community knew her. In the last four years, my health and mobility have started to decline—the result of aging with HIV and the effects of radiation therapy all those years ago—so I retired from work. I couldn't walk as far as I used to, but Hope loved to ride in the car. So we'd cruise downtown and have lunch together, and then I'd take her to her favorite pet store for a treat.

She motivated me to get out of the shell I'd developed over all the years of being sick and helped me reestablish my place in the world.

It's been a rough road. I'm sixty-two and I look at other long-term HIV survivors and sometimes think, *Wow, I really got hit with it, didn't I?* There have been countless times over the years when I thought I couldn't do it anymore. Even on days when it felt like my body might give out from under me, having Hope to come home to always made recovery feel within reach.

Hope passed away on March 20, 2019. Except for the death of my father, saying goodbye to her has been the most difficult thing I've ever had to do.

I always assumed Hope would outlive me. She was my child, my little girl—I birthed her. She came into this world in my arms, and she left in my arms. It was an incredibly spiritual experience from beginning to end. Hope was an incredible companion; her unconditional love and dedication were profound. I hope this story can memorialize her in some way.

When Dogs Heal

ROB & FRED

ate in 2010, I woke up in a hospital bed with no recollection of how I'd gotten there. When I learned what had happened—that I'd been assaulted the previous night—I was overcome with grief at being violated. I felt ashamed and disconnected.

A month later, I came down with a horrible flu that lasted longer than it should have, and I thought, *This is HIV.* When I was well enough to return to work at the hospital, I went straight into my office, shut off the lights, locked the door and tested myself. When it came up positive, I ran to my doctor in tears, hoping a blood test would give a different result, but it didn't. In that moment, I felt like my life was over.

I kept both the secret of my diagnosis and the secret of my assault largely locked away for more than a year, because I was paralyzed by shame. I had been blessed with a strong support network, but the stigma that I'd so often seen paired with HIV made me doubt that even my closest friends and family would accept me.

I realize now how completely ironic it was that I had devoted my life to helping others navigate exactly this situation. As a doctor, I'd helped hundreds of young people confront and overcome an HIV diagnosis and its stigma. I started while in medical school at NYU, as an HIV test counselor when people were dying of AIDS left and right. Once, while on call in 1990, I had close to twenty patients die of AIDS in just one night. My next-door neighbor in college got a cold, went to the hospital, and I never saw him again. That kind of stuff happened. The stigma back then was as big a part of the crisis as the virus itself. People would call the clinic trying to find out if their neighbors were HIV positive because nobody wanted to be associated with it or live near it. It's hard to comprehend today just how devastating HIV was for a generation of young people.

On some level, I knew I especially should have been able to overcome the diagnosis and the stigma, but I couldn't. When it was looking me in the face, I couldn't afford myself that same compassion. Instead, it felt like I was crumbling.

Surrounded by my family at Christmas that year, I felt isolated with my pain. I could sense that they suspected something was wrong. Sure enough, before I left, my mom put her hands on my face, looked me straight in the eyes, and said, "You can keep telling me that everything's okay, but I know it's not. One day you'll tell me, and things will get better."

I wished I could have accepted that. I cried the entire flight back home to Chicago, and when I reached my empty apartment, the hopelessness set in. I sat on my bed, wondering whether I could make it to the next day.

I'm not sure where it came from—maybe because I had just been around my brother's dogs over the holidays—but I had a crazy thought: *Maybe I should get a dog.* When I called a friend to tell him my idea, he said, "You can't even take care of yourself. How are you going to take care of a dog?" I knew he was right—I had never taken care of a dog before, let alone owned one—but the more I sat with it, the more I felt hopeful. I looked into it anyway.

I Googled "puppy Chicago," and up popped photos of a litter of Yorkies. I wrote to the owner, who sent me a video. In it, a little puppy was chewing on a plastic knife toy that his littermates kept trying to take from him—he wouldn't give it up. All he wanted, I thought, was to play in peace. A part of me connected with his determination.

Within forty-eight hours, Fred was in my living room. I picked him up in the middle of one of Chicago's infamous snowstorms, so the two of us were stuck in my apartment for three days with no way out. I had no idea what to do with him, so I reached out for advice. Friends told me to have him sleep alone in the bathroom with a blanket that first night to break his anxiety. I tried to do as they said. I put Fred in the bathroom and went into my bedroom down the hall. As he cried, yelped and whined, I tried the TV, I tried the stereo, I tried headphones. I tried everything to take my mind off him until finally I said to myself, *I just took this two-month-old puppy away from his mother and all his siblings. Maybe I can break him of his anxiety tomorrow.*

I took down the doggie gate, Fred ran into my bed, and he's slept in my bed ever since.

Almost every night since the assault, I had woken up before morning, screaming from night terrors. When Fred saw that for the first time, he got so scared that he ran under the bed to hide. I felt awful. I spent the next two hours lying on the floor alongside the bed, telling him how much I loved him, until he finally felt safe enough to come out. Fred was maybe two pounds at the time, so he was no actual threat to an invader, but I felt safer with him there. Soon, the night terrors went from every night to every other night to twice a week to once a month. Now I rarely have them at all.

Fred's energy started to act as a check against mine. If I came home wound up, he wouldn't engage with it. Instead, he maintained a look that seemed to say, *Dial it back, Rob. You're at an eight, and I need you at a three.*

What's proved most important, though, is that Fred has no tolerance for isolation. There were times I wanted to stay holed up in my apartment, but Fred needed me to take him out, and I couldn't take him outside without half of Boystown wanting to pet and talk to him. Half the time, I'd think, "Ugh, I just want to go home," but over time those little bits of interaction reconnected me.

As we both grew, he increasingly required me to be present. If we were walking, and I got on my phone, he'd stop and stick a paw up and look at me, as if to remind me that it was *his* time and he would not have me distracted during it. Or if we were watching TV together and I reached for my phone, he growled. If I was on my computer too late at night and got up to go to the kitchen, he closed my laptop. At times I couldn't help but laugh, but he seemed to know I needed a constant reminder of what is really important in life.

This isn't to say everything's gone right for me since Fred showed up. Over the years, I've struggled with addiction and other destructive tendencies. But Fred has shown me that addiction and disengagement go hand in hand. The more he forces me to go out and be social and enjoy the simple moments, the less I struggle. And my shame around my HIV status goes out the window too. Fred is the antithesis to disconnection, and what he's given me has been profound.

I generate a lot of self-worth from my work. It's much easier to channel my energy into my patients than it is to devote my time and energy to self-care. I've often feared downtime, because that's when anxiety comes rushing in—followed by doubt, self-loathing and loneliness. In the years since my diagnosis, I've fought demons both external and internal. The external ones—the people who assaulted me—are gone from my life in the physical sense. It's the internal ones—the shame and fear planted by their assault—that have festered and grown.

For a while, I lost a part of myself to that. But Fred filled that space with love and joy and reminded me that secrecy has never been my friend—whether it was my sexuality, HIV or addiction. All it does is give the secret more power. For a lot of people in this book, myself included, an HIV diagnosis is still linked to shame, and shame breeds isolation. But when you decide to bring a dog into your life, you can't stay isolated for long. Dogs require you to engage with the world, to get off your couch and out of your house and as a result get out of the dark.

Deciding to start Fred Says in 2012 was the first time I thought, *I'm going to take back control.* I had this magical animal who brought light back to my life, and I wanted to share that with the world. It was then that I started to disclose my status to others.

It was funny. Even as I told friends, I'd built up a lot of my anxiety around telling my mom. When I came out to her as a gay man, the one thing she was afraid of was that I was going to get HIV, and that lingered in the back of my mind. Yet when the moment actually came to tell her, she barely blinked an eye about my status. All she cared about was that somebody had hurt me. The next time I visited New Jersey, I left Fred with my mom for a while. I came back to find her in the kitchen holding Fred, crying and whispering, "You brought my son back."

Fred is a miracle of a dog, but he's not a miracle worker. I don't want anyone to believe my dog is a panacea. Healing requires my participation, and we work on it together. Over the last eight years, Fred has been my partner in crime, my copilot and my guardian angel. He's shown me an unconditional love that I don't think is possible from a human. People internalize hurt and have a hard time moving on, but not dogs. I have not always been the best father, but no matter what kind of father I am, Fred is always there for me. When you're grappling with an HIV diagnosis, there is no way to overstate the importance of that kind of support.

Fred reminds me that there's more to life than work. I can't take work with me when I go, and it's never going to love me back. When I go to sleep at night, and Fred curls up in my arms and I feel that he is at peace, I know that my job for the day is done.

FRED SAYS: IT ALL STARTED WITH A DOG!

Fred, a Yorkshire terrier, was born on October 24, 2010—the same year Dr. Robert Garofalo was diagnosed with HIV. With his life in crisis and unsure where to turn for love and support, Rob adopted Fred at just two months old, in hopes of companionship and an escape from the trauma and isolation of his diagnosis. Within months, Fred proved to be an invaluable source of healing.

With Fred by his side, Rob felt newly inspired to make the world a better place for others affected by HIV/AIDS. He created a grassroots, self-sustaining charity called Fred Says that supports young people living with HIV across the United States and in Nigeria. Since 2013, the Fred Says foundation has given more than $300,000 to the HIV community, supporting the education of young people living with HIV and organizations working with and supporting HIV-positive youth. Among the organizations that have received financial support are:

Advocates for Youth, Washington, DC
Ann & Robert H. Lurie Children's Hospital, Chicago, IL
Bay Area Young Positives (Bay Positives), San Francisco, CA
Broadway Youth Center of Howard Brown Health, Chicago, IL
Callen-Lorde Community Health Center, New York, NY
Children's Hospital of Los Angeles—HIV program, Los Angeles, CA
Los Angeles LGBT Center via AIDS/LifeCycle, Los Angeles, CA
Lost-n-Found Youth, Atlanta, GA
Pridelines Youth Programs, Miami, FL
Southwest Center for HIV/AIDS, Phoenix, AZ
TPAN (Test Positive Aware Network), Chicago, IL
University of Ibadan Youth HIV Program, Ibadan, Nigeria

Fred Says has supported a number of educational scholarships for youth affected by HIV in both the United States and Nigeria, and it recently launched a dog adoption and wellness program called Paws N' Effect in partnership with Chicago's TPAN organization.

Fred Says is recognized by the US federal government as a 501(c)(3) nonprofit charitable organization. To support HIV-positive youth through Fred Says, please visit its website: www.fredsays.org.

PAWS N' EFFECT

Paws N' Effect is the first initiative in the United States to successfully address mental health and the role it plays in treatment adherence for people living with HIV. Chicago-based nonprofits TPAN, Fred Says and Felines & Canines animal shelter launched the program in 2019.

Paws N' Effect pairs people struggling with isolation, depression and anxiety as a result of their HIV diagnosis with a dog in need of a home. In each of the five matches its first year, the simple yet profound connection between patient and shelter dog has improved how clients feel, function and engage in their health care.

Julie Supple, TPAN's director of client services, and Rob Garofalo, founder of the Fred Says foundation and member of the TPAN board of directors, worked together to create Paws N' Effect. "The power and magnitude of loving and caring for a dog is what makes Paws N' Effect so important," says Julie. "It gives our clients the ability to [build a] relationship that will likely change their lives forever and for the better."

"This program is a labor of love," says Garofalo, who has seen the fruits of canine companionship in his own health-care regimen, as well as in those of his patients. "We have only recently begun to fully understand the power of the human-animal bond, and our hope is that this program will become a model for other communities across the country."

Abby Smith, executive director of Felines & Canines, has placed hundreds of support animals with patients over the years. "I have seen firsthand how it can change somebody's life," she says.

In 2019 Paws N' Effect paired an HIV-positive client battling loneliness and isolation with a dog named Josie. Josie's previous owner had died of cancer, and she was both anxious and traumatized. "It's going so beautifully," said the client. "I'm spoiling her. We both feel safer because we have each other. We've just become so close. French fries are her favorite snack!"

Mental health therapist Dayna Flores notes a dramatic change in HIV-positive clients after they participate in Paws N' Effect. "Since my client received her pup, I've noticed a new motivation for her to engage and participate in life," she observed. "Before, she often spoke about feeling lonely, isolated and misunderstood. Now she focuses more on building relationships and exploring the world with a canine companion who provides her with comfort and unconditional love."

Everyone involved has seen evidence of the magical bond between HIV-positive patients and shelter dogs. The transformation and hope developing within Paws N' Effect has changed the lives of each participant—both human and canine—for the better.

For more information about Paws N' Effect, contact Julie Supple at (773) 632-5540 or Dayna Flores at (773) 632-5583.

RESOURCES

Advocates for Youth helps young people make informed and responsible decisions about their reproductive and sexual health. The website provides a full range of education and information about HIV, including information fact sheets on prevention strategies such as condoms and pre-exposure prophylaxis (PrEP).
https://advocatesforyouth.org/

AIDSVu is an easy-to-use online tool that helps people learn more about the HIV epidemic in the United States. The Find Services tab helps you locate HIV testing, pre-exposure prophylaxis (PrEP) and HIV care services near you.
https://aidsvu.org/

The Centers for Disease Control and Prevention is a comprehensive resource for educational information on the epidemiology of HIV in the United States; HIV transmission, prevention, and testing; and treatment and living with HIV. The website includes a geographical service provider to find nearby HIV testing, pre-exposure prophylaxis (PrEP), post-exposure prophylaxis (PEP) and condoms.
https://www.cdc.gov/hiv/basics/index.html
https://gettested.cdc.gov/

HealthHIV works with organizations, communities and health-care providers to advance effective prevention, care and support for people living with, or at risk for, HIV and HCV. Resources include education and training, technical assistance, advocacy, and health services research and evaluation. The website includes a national online directory providing consumers and organizations with a comprehensive, updated resource of AIDS service organizations and community-based organizations in their geographic area.
https://healthhiv.org/

The Trevor Project is the leading national organization providing crisis intervention and suicide prevention services to lesbian, gay, bisexual, transgender, queer and questioning (LGBTQ) young people under twenty-five. They have a national 24/7 suicide and crisis intervention online and telephone hotline.
https://www.thetrevorproject.org/
(866) 488-7386

ACKNOWLEDGMENTS

Everyone on the *When Dogs Heal* team would like to give a sincere thank-you to Joseph Varisco for his longtime participation in this project and amazing advocacy and coordination during our Chicago shoot. David Hackett and Chuck Hillock were instrumental in our final shoot as well. Thanks to Isaac Barba, Valeda Stull and Michelle Lopez for their assistance. We are grateful for the support of the Ann & Robert H. Lurie Children's Hospital for letting us turn their beautiful new waiting room into a photography studio. Thanks to Dr. Ralph Freidin for introducing Dr. Robert Garofalo to his son's dog photography so many years ago—the beginning of a long and wonderful friendship. Christina would like to thank the brave people who entrusted her with their stories—it has been an honor to share them—and Mario for his unwavering support through the writing process. Thanks also to Anna Olswanger, whose belief in this book never wavered, and to the amazing and passionate team at Lerner Publishing Group. Most importantly, Jesse, Rob, Christina and Zach have felt deeply honored, inspired by and grateful for everyone who willingly reached out to sit for a portrait and share their story of struggle and triumph with us over the years. This book is a testament to your strength of spirit.

Stogie, Trin, Jack, Elly, Max, Pancake, Fred and all the dogs who have provided a shoulder to cry on—or at least a snoot to boop—thank you.

ABOUT THE CONTRIBUTORS

JESSE FREIDIN is America's leading fine art dog photographer. For the past fifteen years his portraiture has studied the deeply healing power of the human-animal bond, telling a contemporary story of companionship and love that truly honors the role dogs play in our lives. Jesse's dog portraits are in private collections throughout the United States and have been exhibited in galleries from coast to coast. His photography has appeared in *Vogue, Cosmopolitan*, the *New York Times*, Huffington Post, and many more. He is the author of *Finding Shelter: Portraits of Love, Healing and Survival* published by Lyons Press in 2017, as well as the Doggie Gaga Project—a personal project that became an overnight media sensation. He works with clients in Santa Fe, San Francisco, and beyond. For information on booking a fine art dog photography session, please visit www.jessefreidin.com.

ZACH STAFFORD is an award-winning journalist, editor, and television host. Most recently he worked as the anchor of the BuzzFeed News morning show *AM to DM* and the editor in chief of the *Advocate* magazine. Prior to these roles, he served as the chief content officer of Grindr and editor in chief of *INTO*, the award-winning LGBTQ digital magazine. He has also served as the editor-at-large of *Out* magazine and was an award-winning journalist at the *Guardian*. Zach regularly provides commentary on radio and podcasts and has appeared on the BBC, CNN, and the *Daily Show with Trevor Noah*. He is the coeditor of the book *Boys, An Anthology* and creator of the documentary *Boystown*. In 2019, he was named to the *Forbes* 30 Under 30 list and to the Root's list of the 100 most influential African Americans.

CHRISTINA GAROFALO is an LA-based TV writer and journalist. She's covered travel, food, and culture for more than a dozen publications, including *Afar*, Huffington Post, *Jetsetter, Paste, Resident, Robb Report,* and ShermansTravel. She's served as an editor for ShermansTravel, *Robb Report,* and Gilt.com. Christina is also the voice of Fred Says on social media. This is her first book.

ROB GAROFALO has devoted his career to caring for adolescents living with HIV. He is a physician and the professor of pediatrics at Northwestern's Feinberg School of Medicine as well as the division head of adolescent medicine at Ann & Robert H. Lurie Children's Hospital of Chicago. Rob codirects the Lurie Children's Hospital Gender Identity & Sex Development Program and is a national authority on the health care of LGBT youth and youth living with HIV. Rob has led several HIV prevention research projects funded by the National Institutes of Health and the Centers for Disease Control and Prevention. Rob founded Fred Says, a nonprofit charity that supports organizations across the US that care for HIV-positive youth. He named the charity after his dog Fred, whom he credits for saving his life after his own HIV-positive diagnosis.